W9-DIW-335

WOMAN'S WORK
The Story of Betty Friedan

WOMAN'S WORK
The Story of Betty Friedan

Lisa Frederiksen Bohannon

MORGAN
REYNOLDS
Publishing, Inc.

620 South Elm Street, Suite 223
Greensboro, North Carolina 27406
http://www.morganreynolds.com

WOMAN'S WORK: THE STORY OF BETTY FRIEDAN

Library of Congress Cataloging-in-Publication Data

Bohannon, Lisa Frederiksen.
  Woman's Work : The Story of Betty Friedan / Lisa Frederiksen Bohannon.
    p. cm.
  Includes bibliographical references and index.
  ISBN 1-931798-41-9 (library binding)
  1. Friedan, Betty. 2. Feminists—United States—Biography—Juvenile liter=
ature. 3. Feminism—United States—History—Juvenile literature. I. Title.=

  HQ1413.F75A3 2004
    305.42'092—dc22

                            2004008444

Printed in the United States of America
First Edition

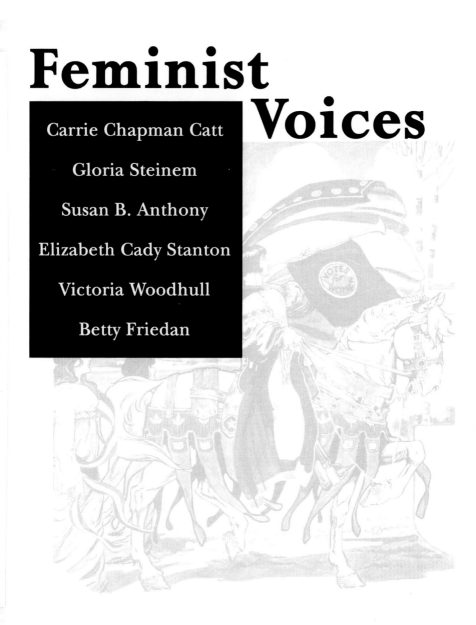

Feminist Voices

Carrie Chapman Catt

Gloria Steinem

Susan B. Anthony

Elizabeth Cady Stanton

Victoria Woodhull

Betty Friedan

For my daughters, Kathryn Marie and
Jessica Erin Scott, with love and admiration

Contents

Betty Friedan
(© AP/WideWorld.)

Chapter One

Growing Up a Goldstein

Every night before bed, ten-year-old Betty Goldstein recited the *Shema Yisrael,* the traditional Jewish evening prayer. She followed it with another familiar bedtime prayer, "Now I lay me down to sleep. God bless Mother and Daddy, and Amy and Harry, and Rex, our dog." Betty's mother had told her and her sister and brother that it was okay to ask God for personal wishes, and over the years, Betty's had included wishes for a bike at Christmas (although Jewish, the family celebrated Christmas) and an end to her dreaded piano lessons. It was during her eleventh year that Betty's bedtime wishes took on a more grown-up appeal. Betty began asking God to grant her wishes for "[a] boy that likes me best . . . [and] . . . a work to do" when she grew up.

Betty's first wish was prompted by her skipping a grade in school and her desire to fit in with her new, older friends. They all seemed to have a boy who liked them best, and Betty wanted one of her own. Her second wish was the result of having grown up in the Goldstein household. Even though she was only ten, Betty felt that she knew what was wrong with her mother, "why she made our life so miserable, my father, us kids, *me* especially, and why, inside, she was so miserable herself." Betty believed the cause of her mother's discontent was that she had no work of her own to do.

Miriam Horwitz, Betty's mother, was born in 1898 and was groomed to be a wife and mother. Upper- and middle-class women did not have jobs or careers in her era. It was just assumed that girls from these families aspired to be good wives and mothers and that good wives and mothers were content with their lives.

Dr. Horwitz, Betty's grandfather, was Hungarian and had been orphaned as a young boy. He had planned to follow in the footsteps of his father, grandfather, and great grandfather, and become a rabbi, but the late 1800s were not a particularly good time for Jewish people living in Eastern Europe. Millions of impoverished non-Jews blamed their Jewish countrymen for the desperate conditions under which they all lived. They organized pogroms on Jewish settlements, attacking and destroying crops, animals, homes, businesses, and even entire families.

Betty's grandfather immigrated to the United States in the 1880s to escape this terror. He decided to become a doctor instead of pursing his rabbinical studies, and put himself through medical school. After serving as a lieutenant colonel in the U.S. Army medical corps in WWI, he married and devoted himself to building a private

Betty's father, Harry Goldstein. *(Courtesy of The Schlesinger Library, Radcliffe Institute, Harvard University.)*

practice while working as Peoria, Illinois's first Public Health Commissioner. Dr. Horwitz became an immigrant success story, a self-made man.

His soon-to-be son-in-law, Harry Goldstein, was also a self-made man. His family had also immigrated to America to escape the pogroms. They had settled in St. Louis, but the promise of a better life soon disappeared as thirteen children crowded into the Goldsteins' home and the family struggled to survive. Harry, the oldest child, struck out on his own at the age of thirteen. He settled in Peoria, where he first earned money peddling buttons on a street corner.

Harry saved his earnings and opened Goldstein Jewelry Company on South Adams Street, two blocks off Peoria's Main Street, in 1908. He advertised it as the "Finest Jewelry Store in the Middle West." The store was a success and he settled into the life of a prosperous businessman. Tragedy stuck when his first wife died of leukemia early in their marriage.

Harry was living as a widower in a luxury apartment in Peoria's Jefferson Hotel when he met Miriam Horwitz. Not yet twenty years old, she worked as the women's page editor for the local newspaper. She had recently graduated with an Associate of Arts degree in Literature from Peoria's Bradley Polytechnic Institute, a combination high school and junior college. Although she had wanted to continue her studies at Smith College, Miriam's parents had refused to send her. They thought she had received all the education she needed.

Dr. and Mrs. Horwitz objected to a romance between Harry and their only child. Harry had little formal education and was not a professional (a doctor, lawyer, or banker). He spoke with a heavy accent and was eighteen years older than Miriam. The fact that he was well read and owned a thriving business did little to improve his standing in their eyes. Miriam was a determined, strong-willed young woman, however, and she married Harry Goldstein against her parent's wishes on February 3, 1920. One friend later explained, "She married him because he was established."

Harry insisted Miriam quit her job at the newspaper because socially prominent married women did not work. After leaving her job, Miriam devoted her energy towards what most upper- and middle-class married women did—establishing a position for her family within Peoria's social circles.

Betty's mother, Miriam. *(Courtesy of The Schlesinger Library, Radcliffe Institute, Harvard University.)*

In the 1920s, Peoria had a population of one hundred thousand, making it the second largest city in Illinois. Located 170 miles southwest of Chicago on the Illinois River, its prominence was due to its position as a manufacturing and transportation hub, connecting Peoria's farming-equipment manufacturers and distilleries with worldwide markets via Chicago to the northeast and the Mississippi River to the west.

Social position in cities like Peoria depended on one's race, religion, and wealth. Miriam was determined the Goldsteins would secure a respectable place. She gave birth to the couple's first child, a daughter they named Bettye Naomi Goldstein, on February 4, 1921—less than six months after the ratification of the Nineteenth Amendment to the U.S. Constitution, granting women the right to vote. Miriam and Harry added an "e" to Betty's name on her birth certificate because it was a fashionable naming practice in the early 1920s. They used it again eighteen months later when they named their second daughter, Amye. Both later dropped the extra letter. Harry Junior, the third and last Goldstein child, arrived in 1926, when Betty was five years old.

Betty was a sickly child. She had to wear iron braces to straighten her bowed legs and spent long periods of her early winters confined to bed with bouts of bronchitis, which later developed into asthma. She was a lovely girl with large brown eyes and dark hair, but her mother made it clear that she did not think Betty was nearly as pretty as her sister. Betty's face, she said, was marred by the prominent nose she had inherited from her father.

Miriam Goldstein considered appearances to be very important. "Our mother always looked as if she had just stepped out of Bergdorf's window," Amy later recalled, "people turned around in the streets. She felt she was a fashion leader. She prided herself that people were imitating her, and this was very important to her." Betty recalled that everything her mother did, "she did perfectly—perfect grooming, her clothes perfectly tailored, meals cooked and served to perfection under her orders." And, of course, she decorated her house to perfection, too. She also swam, played bridge, mahjong, tennis, and

Young Betty. *(Courtesy of The Schlesinger Library, Radcliffe Institute, Harvard University.)*

golf—all important skills for the wife of a socially prominent businessman to have.

Miriam and Harry's social climb took a big step up in
1924 when they moved the family to the West Bluffs.

Betty was three years old. The West Bluffs housed some of Peoria's most prestigious neighborhoods and overlooked the Illinois River Valley and the area where Peoria's poor lived.

The Goldstein family could only move so far up the social ladder, though. The anti-Semitism their ancestors had fled in Europe was present, if to a lesser degree, in 1920s America, too. Because they were Jewish, even an address in the Bluffs was not enough to gain them admittance to the Peoria Country Club, the ultimate symbol of social status. Nor did living in the Bluffs mean they were invited to the homes of the businessmen with whom Harry belonged to Peoria's Chamber of Commerce. When these men locked their doors and closed shop at the end of the workday, Harry Goldstein ceased to exist in their Anglo-Saxon, Protestant world. This treatment humiliated Harry, and to top it off, at home, Miriam constantly belittled him for his lack of education and his accent, as if these were somehow the cause of the Goldsteins' lack of acceptance.

Miriam, embittered by the snubs, pressed ahead with her social-climbing efforts. She set to work settling the family into the three-storied, eight-room, red brick house at 105 Farmington Road that sat atop a hill overlooking Bradley Park. The Goldsteins' new home was perfect for Miriam's weekly luncheons and the afternoon bridge parties she would throw for twenty or so of her friends. She installed a baby grand Steinway piano to grace one corner of the formal living room, which also boasted a gaming table for playing cards and backgammon. In the dining room, thick, cream-colored draperies framed the richly carved table and its accompanying posh, blue upholstered chairs. The elegant color had been selected to complement the room's blue and rose Oriental carpet.

Meals were prepared by a cook and served by a maid who also did the housekeeping. A nurse took care of Betty, Amy, and Harry, and a chauffeur drove the family on special occasions and served as the butler for evening affairs hosted in the Goldstein home.

By the time Betty began school in 1926, the family had settled into a routine. Every morning they rose at seven, and Betty and Amy raced to dress so they could join their father on his morning walk through Bradley Park before he headed to his store. Betty later recalled those walks as some of her fondest early childhood memories.

When Betty's father returned from the shop at the end of the day, the family gathered in the formal dining room for dinner. Miriam sat at the head of the table and Harry at its foot. From her post, she summoned the maid to serve the various courses the cook had prepared. In the early days she used a bell, but later she would have a buzzer installed under the carpet at her feet, and then she could surreptitiously summon the food with a touch of her toe. According to Betty, "At the dinner table, we each would tell what we had done that day, and my father would give us little lectures on important developments, like Lindy crossing the Atlantic."

Even the Goldsteins' summer vacations followed a routine. Every year, Betty's mother would drive the children to a fishing camp at a lake in Wisconsin or Minnesota. Betty later described fighting with her brother and sister on these annual drives, over which one of them got the privilege of sitting in the front seat with their mother. Their father, who would only take off two weeks from the store each year, would join them later.

The rest of the year, while her father was at work, Betty and her siblings took their cues from their mother. "My mother, to all of us, was the most important person in the house. If she was in a good mood, everything was fine. If she was in a bad mood, . . . we all shrank from her, were miserable, and tried to keep out of her way," said Betty.

Betty remembered her mother as being in a bad mood most of the time. Though Miriam taught religion classes at the synagogue, participated in women's groups, and had her bridge parties, luncheons, and volunteer work, "she never had anything that she thought was important to do," Betty said, many years later. That was why, in Betty's opinion, her mother spent much of her life angry and unhappy. Betty even thought that the colitis her mother developed, which sent her to bed with excruciating abdominal pain when her anger and frustrations overtook her, was another of the many consequences of not having a job of her own.

If her mother was not taking her frustrations out on her children, she took them out on their father. Betty recalled her mother constantly ridiculing his failure to earn the amounts of money she wanted to spend. Miriam would hide the bills she had charged and at times try investing in the stock market or gambling in order to cover the debts she had run up. The results were loud fights between her parents after the children had gone to bed; fights which kept Betty awake long into the night.

Books and school provided Betty with an escape from the tensions in the Goldstein household. She learned to read at a very early age and began checking out books six at a time from the library. She'd plop on the floor of the living room, reading on her stomach while "the rest of the family would walk over" her. Her parents soon realized that forbidding her to read was a far more effective punishment than spanking her.

Betty's mother supported her love of reading, and one Christmas she gave Betty all six books in the Honey Bunch series. Betty read every one of them that day. Her mother also gave her a membership in a monthly junior book club and presented her with books for birthday gifts, as well. Betty loved them all, but especially enjoyed the Nancy Drew series, *The Little Colonel, The Little Princess, Little Women,* and *Alice in Wonderland.*

School provided another escape for Betty. "At school I came alive," she said. "School was my safe place, school was my relief, school I loved." Betty was a natural leader, too. When she was in the third grade, she started a group called the Baddy Baddy Club. Everyone not in the club was a 'goody goody.' Club members prided themselves on the pranks they pulled to disrupt class, like shoving their books onto the floor, for example, when Betty gave them the cue.

After school Betty and her friends often gathered at

her house for make-believe games. They donned her mother's old hats, dresses, shoes, and coats to play the parts of movie stars, spies, princesses, detectives, and villains, and strung blankets from the water pipes and rafters to create a stage.

Betty joined the Girl Scouts and she loved going to camp, where she could hike, explore, and canoe. She treasured her time outdoors and the escape it provided from the dreaded swimming, tennis, golf, and piano lessons that her mother insisted upon. "I wasn't good at any of it," said Betty. "Nothing I did was ever right, ever satisfied her." Amy, on the other hand, excelled at all of it.

Betty rebelled by taking a stand against everything her mother stood for. She deliberately neglected her appearance and developed rude and blunt behavior. She ridiculed the social activities her mother engaged in and made sure never to engage in them herself.

Miriam never stopped trying to change Betty, however, and she persevered in her efforts to position the Goldstein family in Peoria's most prominent social circles. She had made great strides by the time Betty's eighth birthday arrived in 1929. Miriam even convinced Betty's father to move the family to a more prestigious address in the Bluffs, some ten blocks from their house on Farmington Road. Life was good. Then, suddenly, the Goldsteins' world, and that of most Americans, collapsed after the stock market crashed on October 24, 1929—a day that came to be known as Black Tuesday because of the social and economic devastation that followed.

Chapter Two

Lonely in Peoria

More than thirteen million Americans lost their jobs in the three years after Black Tuesday. Thousands of businesses went bankrupt. Americans who did find work were paid far less than ever before, some as little as ten cents an hour. Most could not afford to keep their personal belongings, and millions lost their homes and life savings in the wake of some ten thousand bank failures that followed the stock market crash. This period in American history, known as the Great Depression, lasted until the late 1930s.

The Goldstein Jewelry Company was hard hit by the Great Depression. Luxury items were no longer on most people's shopping lists, but Harry refused to close his store or declare bankruptcy. He was concerned for his employees' well-being and managed to keep the store running in order to pay their wages. The strain took its toll on his health, though, and before long, he was suffering from hypertension and heart trouble. These conditions worsened as the fighting between Harry and Miriam over money became fiercer. The dinner table was a favorite battleground. When husband and wife began using their children to needle each other, it only exacerbated the strain on Betty and her siblings. Betty was her father's favorite. Intrigued by her brilliant mind (she scored 180 on an IQ test), he directed his dinner conversations to her, effectively excluding his wife and the other children, who were not interested in following their conversations. Betty's mother adored Harry Jr., and Amy held a special place in her heart, as well; she had inherited her mother's natural beauty and social grace. Betty's mother would comment on the differences between Betty and her siblings, praising their successes and voicing her disappointment over Betty's failures. Yet there were times when Miriam would enlist all three children to join her side. Betty's mother "created a kind of conspiracy with us, to keep it a secret from Daddy that she had bought something, a dress for one of us or for herself, something for the house. And I was part of that conspiracy which made Daddy the enemy." It was a terribly confusing situation that perpetuated Betty's sense of loneliness.

Once again, Betty turned to school and friends for solace. She had advanced a grade in school when she was ten. In order to make new friends she created a club that she called the JFF—the Just For Fun club. Boys and girls were admitted and Friday night was club night. They would gather to listen to records, drink sodas, or sled down the snow-covered hills in Bradley Park. Betty was optimistic about starting junior high in the fall of 1932.

Junior high school was exciting. Betty and her friends continued their fun times by roller skating, going to movies, and taking turns throwing dance parties. She tried out for a writing position with *The Reflector,* the school's newspaper, "as my mother made sure I would," she said. Though Betty later speculated it was her mother's way of reliving her own unfulfilled dreams of being a writer, she nonetheless found that she loved newspapers.

Betty also convinced her mother to let her substitute acting lessons for the piano lessons she hated so much. Soon Betty was trying out for child parts with the Peoria Players, the local amateur theater company. She was talented enough to land some parts. "I loved hanging around that theater," she said. She had discovered another way to cope with her chaotic home life: keeping busy.

Though her parents, especially her mother, were neither devout nor Orthodox in their religious observances, they did carry on many of the Jewish traditions. When Betty turned twelve, she began preparing for her Bat Mitzvah (her confirmation) in the Anshai Emeth Temple. Betty studied Hebrew and the Torah in preparation. Shortly before she was scheduled to be confirmed, though, she informed the rabbi, "I've decided I don't believe there is a God." He calmly received the news and told her to "keep it to [her]self until after confirmation." Betty followed his advice. She later recalled, "I soulfully raised my eyes to the heavens and spoke the prayer, good actress that I was, as if I was a candidate for Jewish sainthood."

With her confirmation and thirteenth birthday behind her, Betty anxiously awaited the start of high school in the fall of 1934. She was conscious of looking a lot younger than her fellow female classmates. Most of them "were getting breasts and periods and wearing brassieres and high heels, and I was still flat-chested, wearing white socks and patent leather Mary Janes," she recalled. Nevertheless, school was her haven, and it had been a long summer cooped up in the Goldstein household.

From the start, things did not go well for Betty in high school. Central High School, the oldest high school in Peoria, was forced to run two shifts of class schedules due to overcrowding. All of the members of Betty's JFF club were in the morning shift, with classes from eight in the morning until two in the afternoon. Betty was in the afternoon shift and her classes met from nine-thirty until three-thirty. Though she found the subjects of French, Latin, Algebra, Geometry far more interesting and challenging than those she had taken in junior high, she could not revive the social world she and her friends had inhabited just months before:

> I would walk to high school alone, eat lunch alone, walk home from high school after four, and sometimes the others would pass me, in their souped-up jalopies, on the way to Hunt's, the drive-in hamburger stand at the foot of Farmington Road, for Cokes or root beer floats, hot dogs or hamburgers, and they would be shouting or laughing and maybe not even wave at me. For some unaccountable rea-

son—some terrible mystery of fate—I had dropped out of their world. Sometimes I would make a detour and go into the cemetery on the street behind our house and sit on a gravestone reading poetry, pretending I was Emily Dickinson. But oh how much I would rather have been in that jalopy going off to Hunt's with my friends.

Betty tried to enter high school society by joining one of Central High's three sororities. These clubs were very popular and most of the members of Betty's JFF Club were included. Betty was not. She was Jewish and Jews were not allowed.

Betty was devastated, shocked, and confused. These had been her close friends just months before, and now they acted as if she did not exist. Betty's mother did not help the situation. "My mother didn't want me to even think of myself as Jewish . . . [instead] something was wrong with *me* that I didn't get into a sorority," she said.

One particularly lonely afternoon, a group of her former friends passed her, crowded into a car. Betty glared after them and swore to herself, "They may not like me, but they are going to have to look up to me."

Resolutely, Betty set out to make other friends who weren't in the sororities. She pushed herself so hard to be extroverted that she often came off as bossy, opinionated, and excessively talkative. Eventually, she found three new friends, Barbara Weir, Harriet Vance, and Janet Jacquin. They, too, were different from the average student at Central High. Barbara's mother was a widow who

Betty with her friends Paul Jordan and Doug Palmer. *(Courtesy of The Schlesinger Library, Radcliffe Institute, Harvard University.)*

ran a travel agency. Janet Jacquin was unusual because she was a Catholic. Harriet Vance, perhaps Betty's closest friend, was also extremely intelligent. "It was not very useful to be too intelligent, for a girl, in Peoria when we were growing up," Betty remembered. Attributes like beauty and charm were more highly prized.

To counter being sidelined by the sorority scene, Betty decided to pick up her pen for the school newspaper, *Opinion.* She wrote book reviews and shared a column byline with another student, John Parkhurst. They addressed issues such as the need for students to reform school politics and offered advice on how to behave courteously at school plays. They also gave as much praise to scholarly achievements as they did to athletic ones. When Betty's book reviews for the *Opinion* were replaced with letters to the editor, Betty, Doug Palmer, Paul Jordan, and two other girls decided to pool their talents and start a literary magazine. They called it *Tide.*

Tide was a sixteen-page publication of poems and stories put together from start to finish by Betty and her co-founders. They did the writing and the layout and sold ads to help cover their expenses. The magazine sold for 10¢ a copy and was hugely successful. *Tide* put Betty back into the limelight. Being a part of Central High's first literary magazine made her feel, once again, like she belonged. "We would walk up Main Street hill, Doug and Paul and I, after putting the magazine to bed in the print shop, and the sun would be setting, and I would feel blissful," she recalled.

Betty's father clipped all of her published columns, poems, and articles and saved them in a safe at his store. He brought them out regularly to share with customers, boasting about his brilliant daughter. Miriam encouraged Betty's writing, as well, though little else about their relationship had changed. "I cannot remember ever being *touched* by her, in the kind of spontaneous hug I delighted in with my own children," she later wrote, and went on, "I must have longed so terribly for that touch."

Harry Goldstein's health continued to decline and gradually Miriam took over the management of the

Goldstein Jewelry Store. Betty noticed a change in her mother even as their relationship became more difficult: "Literally, physically, she stopped having the colitis which all during our childhood would periodically send her to bed, screaming with pain, for days at a time. She stopped picking on us so much. She was too busy. But watching my father decline, I hated my mother. . . . I felt that her demands, the constant battling, the way she sneered at my father for his accent and lack of education, the lack of support in our home—combined with the endless pressures of making the money that was never enough for her, even before and after the Depression—were what was killing him," she said.

Betty's passion for drama and acting, discovered in junior high, carried her through some of these difficult times. It eased the sense of isolation and rejection she felt during her first two years at Central High and provided an outlet for the more lively, outgoing person she pushed herself to become during her last two. Summer jobs and school clubs also helped her escape her home life and Central High's exclusive social scene. One summer she worked in Peoria's settlement house, another as a tutor to a German family who had fled Hitler, and another doing odds jobs at Peoria's newspaper. She joined the Quill and Scroll Club, an honor society for writers; Charvice, the school's honor society; the Junior National Honor Society; and the French, Science, Cue, and Drama Clubs.

Beneath her bravado, however, lurked Betty's deepest desires—for acceptance by the majority of her peers and a boy who liked her best. Her brother said, "When Betty was in high school she was ugly and had no boyfriends. She was popular and well liked—fellows *liked* her. But if a girl didn't get invited to a dance, she felt ostracized." During her final months at Central High, Betty decided to focus her efforts on getting out of Peoria.

She sent college applications to Vassar, Radcliffe, Wellesley, Stanford, the University of Chicago, and Smith, and was admitted to all of them. Even though the University of Chicago had an innovative humanities curriculum that impressed her, she chose to go to Smith, the college of her mother's dreams some twenty years earlier. Chicago was not far enough away from Peoria.

Excited to be moving on, Betty took the stage as one of Central High School's six valedictorians on gradua-

Betty (front row, second from left) in the Quill and Scroll Club's yearbook photo.
(Courtesy of The Schlesinger Library, Radcliffe Institute, Harvard University.)

tion day, June 9, 1938. She was seventeen years old. Her classmates expected she would become a writer, according to the school yearbook. Doug said she was "inordinately ambitious" and would "strive . . . to reach the top of the world." Betty agreed: "I want to do something with my life—to have an absorbing interest. I want success and fame," she said.

Before she left home, Betty and her father had a frank discussion about her relationship with her mother. Betty wanted to know why nothing she did ever seemed to be good enough. Her father looked at Betty and said, "She made it possible for you to have the advantages she didn't have. She couldn't get out of here the way you can now." It would be years before Betty would understand and appreciate her mother's actions. In the meantime, the one thing Betty did understand was that she was getting out of Peoria. She also knew "it was seared deep in my gut that I didn't want to grow up and be like my mother."

Chapter Three

Coming into Her Own

In September 1938, Betty boarded a sleeping car on the train from Chicago to Northampton, Massachusetts, where Smith College is located. Harriet Vance, a good friend of Betty's who had also been accepted to Smith, traveled with her.

Betty found the sixty-three-year-old Smith campus breathtakingly beautiful. Paradise Pond covered one corner of the campus, and great stretches of green lawns, studded with old, canopied trees, lush hedges, and flowering bushes covered the rest. Stately, three-storied brick mansions with tall white columns encased in ivy formed the perimeter of the quad. These mansions provided the housing for Smith's two thousand female students. Betty was assigned to Chapin House.

Life on campus was similar to life in a wealthy home and was governed by decades-old traditions and ceremonies. Maids were employed to make the beds, do the laundry, and serve the meals the cooks prepared. Dining was a formal affair, complete with linens and silver place settings, and appropriate attire was required—no bathrobes, shorts, or other casual wear. There was a smoking room and a lounging room where residents could enjoy a game of bridge or read the newspaper before retiring for the evening. Students were required to attend chapel once a week and to adhere to a ten o'clock curfew. Drinking alcohol was strictly forbidden.

Betty Goldstein was smitten with Smith from the start. She loved her classes in history, philosophy, economics, English, and psychology. She was thrilled to be reading contemporary and classic literature, including Virginia Woolf's *Mrs. Dalloway* and *A Room of One's Own;* Thomas Mann's *The Magic Mountain;* Gustave Flaubert's *Madame Bovary;* and James Joyce's *A Portrait of the Artist as a Young Man.* She started a daily routine of reading newspapers, especially the *New York Times,* and embraced world politics with a passion.

Reading Ernest Hemingway's *For Whom the Bell Tolls* inspired her to do further research on the Spanish Civil War. She studied the Russian Revolution, capitalism, the French Revolution, and the Great Depression, and remembered "passionately arguing in and after philosophy class or history class about communism and fascism, about the war in Europe, about art as pure truth."

Most of all, Betty found acceptance at Smith: "the academic life, the life of the mind, and the life of music and art and theater and writing and social conscience was the important life at Smith, not the small world of social snobbery." What had made her stand out as different from her peers in Peoria now made her one of the crowd. Betty hoped to land a position with the college's newspaper, but was felled by a savage attack of asthma that landed her in the hospital. Her mother was called to her bedside, and back in Peoria, the congregation at the temple prayed for her recovery. The summer before leaving for college, Betty had developed a bad cough that had never fully gone away. These severe asthma attacks would plague her repeatedly over the next several decades, especially during times of stress or when faced with making a major change or important decision.

Despite her poor health, Betty was awarded a position reporting for *The Smith College Weekly* and soon became the paper's news editor. She worked with the editor-in-chief, Joan Marble, to model the paper after the *New York Times*. Together, they turned it into a semi-weekly publication, a production that required the talents and efforts of some eighty students. In the spring of 1941, her junior year, Betty was elected editor-in-chief and she changed the paper's name to the *Smith College Associated News (SCAN)*. She sought and found scores of causes to rail against. She wanted very much to disturb the status quo and to vent her newly found radicalism.

This new radicalism was the result of three events that occurred during her sophomore year and the summer prior to her junior year. The first involved her reading Robert and Helen Lynd's *Middletown in Transition*. Middletown was the code name the Lynds had given to Muncie, Indiana, a city they had studied some ten years before, in the 1920s. In that study, titled *Middletown,* the

Lynds, then affiliated with the Presbyterian faith, had focused on Muncie's religious activities and major institutions. When the Lynds conducted their follow-up study some ten years later, which they titled *Middletown in Transition,* their own values and intellectual predispositions had changed. They had become more aligned with the views of Karl Marx, the German philosopher and radical leader who had founded the modern communist movement. Taking a fresh look at Muncie from their new Marxist perspective convinced the Lynds that the differences in Muncie were really differences in class, not religious faith. Muncie sounded very much like her hometown of Peroria, and Betty began to think about that place in a whole new light.

The second event leading to Betty's radicalization was taking an Economics course called "Theories and Movements for Social Reconstruction," taught by Professor Dorothy Wolff Douglas. Professor Douglas was something of a radical in her own right. She had divorced Professor Paul H. Douglas, who would later become a three-term Senator from Illinois, and was living with her four children and her partner, Katharine Du Pre Lumpkin, when Betty enrolled in her class. Professor Douglas was also Jewish, widely read, a published author, politically active, and radically left in her beliefs. Douglas had visited the Soviet Union to observe, first hand, its communist labor and socialist system.

Douglas thought that strong labor unions and social welfare programs were the key to halting the spread of fascism in Europe, which had already taken hold in Italy,

Germany, and Spain. Fascism is a dictatorial form of government in which the leaders take control of all private enterprises and maintain control by repressing any and all opposition. While Betty was studying economics at Smith, the fascist leaders of Germany and Italy (Adolf Hitler and Benito Mussolini) were leading the Axis powers to a succession of quick victories against the Allied forces fighting World War II.

Betty Goldstein became an ardent anti-fascist under Douglas's tutelage. Douglas was also the first person in Betty's life to voice concern over discrimination against women in the workplace. Professor Douglas deplored the fact that women received lesser wages for work equal to men's. She also criticized society's failure to economically value a woman's contribution to the household economy.

It was Douglas's influence that led to the third major event in the process of Betty's radicalization—an eight week summer internship at the Highlander Folk School in Monteagle, Tennessee. Professor Douglas had recommended Betty for the internship because she recognized her superior intellectual abilities and strong political leanings.

Highlander Folk School was well known for its educational and research programs. Workers, grassroots leaders, community organizers, educators, and researchers gathered to brainstorm about social, environmental, and economic problems and nonviolent ways to effect change. Martin Luther King, Jr. and Rosa Parks would attend workshops at Highlander Folk School a decade later, and

Writing was never an easy process for Betty, shown here at her typewriter. *(Courtesy of The Schlesinger Library, Radcliffe Institute, Harvard University.)*

would use the information and methods gathered there in their roles as leaders of the Civil Rights Movement.

At Highlander, Betty participated in a writer's workshop and a program that taught students about labor unions, workers, and the economy. She wrote a piece titled "Learning the Score," which was a scathing attack on capitalism and social class hierarchies in places such as Peoria. One excerpt read, "My father's friends own the distilleries and banks and office buildings of Peoria. To them the profit of the employer is a sacred right. . . . [They argue that] employees should be grateful. If they try to organize [unions] they are being greedy, they are trying to steal what does not belong to them. If they were any good to begin with, they wouldn't be workers." Their sentiments now appalled and angered Betty.

Betty's experiences at Highlander and in Professor Douglas's class, and her reading of *Middletown in Transition,* left her convinced that strong labor unions and federally sponsored social programs to assist the poor and working classes were needed to prevent the spread of fascism. She returned to Smith for her junior year, in the fall of 1940, politically engaged and determined to use her role as editor-in-chief of *SCAN* to challenge her fellow students.

One of her crusades involved writing an exposé of the secret societies that had been a part of Smith College since the 1890s. Memberships in the secret societies were inherited from Smith alumnae. These exclusive societies reminded Betty of the sororities at Central High School. Another of her causes was to support the campus maids' strike and their drive to unionize. She also wrote articles expressing anti-fascist, pro-peace, and pro-labor-movement positions. *SCAN* also took on Smith's student government for holding closed meetings, published critiques of classes and professors' teaching styles, and campaigned to embarrass the wealthy Smith students for their excesssive consumption when the nation was being asked to sacrifice for the war effort in Europe.

"Whatever came to her attention she became fascinated by. Betty just sopped up learning. She had a brain that could amass material and organize it," said Priscilla Buckley, one of *SCAN*'s assistant editors. Another assistant editor, Sally Gavin, said of Betty, "She was bossy, but I did like her. We were a good group and we had fun together. She did not foster intimacy. It was more of a push-and-push back relationship with Betty." For her part, Betty found working on *SCAN* to be one of the most rewarding experiences of her life. "I loved walking home from the library, the days our newspaper came out, and seeing girls sitting on the steps of the college houses reading the paper, hearing them argue about my editorials," she said.

During her last two years at Smith, Betty decided to focus her studies in psychology. "It fascinated me, obsessed me, scared me. It gave me new words to express my deep uneasiness about my own 'normality' (or craziness)," she said. This concern was the result of having taken the Rorschach test, in which the subject gives her interpretation of ten abstract inkblot designs. The subject's interpretations are then analyzed to determine her emotional and intellectual functioning and integration. According to her test results, Goldstein was "either a hopeless schizophrenic or some test-breaking genius."

Goldstein enrolled in courses covering some of the world's leading psychologists' thinking on a broad spectrum of issues, including learning, cognition, intelligence, motivation, emotion, perception, personality, and mental disorders. One class she took in her junior year, taught by Dr. Kurt Koffka, was a graduate seminar on Gestalt theory. Koffka had co-founded the Gestalt school of psychology, which claimed that the whole is more than just the sum of its parts, that the parts derive their meaning from the whole, and that the whole is affected by an individual's perception, memory, and learning.

The Gestalt principle of closure provides a simple example of the theory's main tenets: when a person is shown a triangle with a small part of its edge missing, that person will generally close the gap and see a complete triangle even though, in reality, it is not complete. For Betty, "the elegant conceptual structure of Gestalt psychology made [her] feel like some kind of mental mountain goat, leaping from peak to peak. . . . And [she] learned, forever, that the whole is more than the sum of its parts, that human behavior can only be understood in its cultural context, that our vision cannot be wholly objective."

The summer following Koffka's class, Betty's psychology professors sent her to Iowa City to work with Kurt Lewin on his experiments with group dynamics. Lewin had developed the discipline of social psychology, which is the study of individuals in their social and cultural settings. His theory was considered radical in 1941, as most psychologists at that time believed human behavior was influenced by internal forces and not by one's surroundings.

When Betty returned to Smith for her senior year in the fall of 1941, she studied the psychology of personality development as set forth by Alfred Adler, Carl Jung, and Sigmund Freud. Freud's work with neurologically disturbed patients had led him to develop his famous theory of psychoanalysis. To help his patients reveal their repressed anxieties and overcome bad experiences, Freud would have the patient lie on a couch facing away from him. From there, he would encourage the patient to use free association to bring their subconscious conflicts to their consciousness. Then he could help with analysis and resolution. This method is known as psychoanalysis.

Freud also developed a theory of personality develop-ment known as the psychosexual stages of development. He argued that at certain points in the human develop-mental process, particular erogenous zones are more sensitive to erotic stimulation than others. These sensi-tivities shift as development progresses. Freud believed that if an individual is not able to satisfy his or her sexual needs during any one of these developmental stages, he or she would not be able to successfully move on to the next stage of personality development. The developmen-tal stages Freud defined were the oral stage, the anal stage, and the phallic stage (the genitals). According to his theories, getting stuck in one of these stages could lead to such conditions as penis envy, anal retention, and oedipal complexes.

Betty's study of psychology, in particular of Gestalt and social psychology theories, helped her to visualize her goals and develop ways of achieving them. At the time, her goals were focused primarily on halting fas-cism and supporting the underdog. The notion, fueled by Gestalt theory, that a change in the individual (the part) could effect a change in society (the whole) was heartening to the twenty-year-old woman.

The psychological theories and practices Betty studied at Smith College would not have even been mentioned, much less studied, in Peoria. She thrived in the freer intellectual atmosphere of Smith, and her professors were continually impressed with her work. She was elected to Phi Beta Kappa, the honor society of American colleges and universities, and to Sigma Xi, the national honor society for the sciences. Her senior thesis, "Operationism in Psychology," was so well received that it was published in a respected scientific journal, the *Psychological Review.*

Yet, in spite of her academic achievements, her acceptance by the majority of her peers, and the power she wielded as *SCAN's* editor-in-chief, Betty still suffered the deep agony of not having regular dates on the weekends, let alone a serious boyfriend. She dated a few times, but the dates never went well. "I was that girl with all A's and I wanted boys worse than anything," she said, "with all that brilliance, I saw myself becoming the old maid college teacher."

Worries over not having a boyfriend were crowded from her mind, however, as she faced the end of her senior year. "I remember the stillness of a spring afternoon on the Smith campus in 1942, when I came to a frightening dead end in my vision of the future…. 'Is this [being a psychologist] really what I want to be?' The question shut me off, cold and alone, from the girls talking and studying on the sunny hillside behind the college house. I thought I was going to be a psychologist. But if I wasn't sure, what did I want to be? I felt the future closing in—and I could not see myself in it at all. I had no image of myself, stretching beyond college," she later explained.

An anxiety attack took hold as she pondered this and other questions. "Nobody had ever really asked me, 'What do you want to be when you grow up, little girl?'" she said. "Even at a college like Smith, women were not expected then to prepare for careers. We were expected to be responsible competent community leaders, good wives and mothers, and cultured patrons of the arts, hostesses for our husbands. I don't think I even heard the word 'career' until 'career women' became a term of opprobrium [scorn or contempt], imbued with nuances of Freudian penis envy."

Betty's relationship with her parents did not help her deal with her angst. Her father's health had deteriorated to the point that he was unable to attend her graduation. She was deeply saddened that he could not be there to watch her receive a college literary prize for her newspaper editorials and to graduate *summa cum laude* with a record-breaking GPA, the highest of any student ever to graduate from Smith, according to the college's president.

Still uncertain as to what she should do following graduation, Betty applied for a coveted fellowship to study for a master's degree in psychology at the University of California at Berkeley (UC Berkeley). After hearing of her acceptance, she was relieved and decided to take an internship in psychology at Grasslands Hospital

Betty's graduation photo, Smith College, 1942. *(Courtesy of The Schlesinger Library, Radcliffe Institute, Harvard University.)*

in Westchester County, New York, for the summer rather than spend it back home in Peoria.

Tucked inside her suitcase, as she boarded the train heading east, were works by Karl Marx and Thorstein Veblen. By the end of her Smith years, Betty's political leanings were decidedly against fascism and for the rights of workers and the need to aid the poor, and she found the theories of these two thinkers particularly fascinating. Veblen, an American economist and social scientist, had written *The Theory of the Leisure Class* in 1899. He had gained fame for coining phrases such as "conspicuous consumption." While Veblen ridiculed the upper classes, he still believed they gave purpose to the lives of the working classes, who he said aspired to climb the social ladder.

Veblen's view contrasted with Karl Marx's "The Communist Manifesto" and *Das Kapital.* Both of these works presented Marx's doctrine, which came to be known as Marxism. In his writings, Marx created a unified theory that he said explained how human history had progressed in the past and how it would develop in the future. Marx's theory combined philosophy with history and economics.

In the Marxist worldview, it was neither ideas nor religion that drove history. Rather, it was the clash of economic classes. The Middle Ages, for example, had been defined by the feudal system when the nobles controlled the land and allowed the peasants to farm it for a price. Marx asserted that under the capitalist economies that were gaining ascendancy at the time he was writing, the wealthy bourgeoisie (or middle class) who owned the factories would be in the dominant position. Workers would, for a while, be left powerless, with no alternative but to work in the factories. At some point in the future, however, the workers would overthrow the bourgeoisie and replace capitalism with a society governed by the workers, where everything was owned communally. This new, classless society would be the end of history because everyone would contribute according to his ability, receive according to his needs, and live as free citizens. In his scenario, there would be no more class conflict because there would be no more class system; everyone would be equal.

These big ideas excited Betty. Armed with the new way of thinking about the world that she had garnered from Veblen and Marx, she felt a nagging pull, a yearning for something more, as she journeyed east. She was in search of something that would recapture the sense of direction and purpose she had felt while attending Smith College.

Chapter Four

Radical Reporter

Shortly after moving to New York in the summer of 1942, Betty learned that a friend from Smith, Liz Roberts, was now living in New York City. Her husband had been a conscientious objector in the war and the editor of the Dartmouth newspaper during his college years. Liz and her husband had become radicals, attending Communist Front study groups, labor union organizing meetings, and political rallies in New York City.

During the late 1930s and early 1940s, American society was fairly accepting of people who professed communist or socialist beliefs. One of America's most important allies in the war against Nazi Germany was the Soviet Union, the first and most dominant Communist country. Many believed that communism and socialism were far better than fascism and also that they were the political systems most likely capable of stopping the spread of fascism in Europe. Additionally, the Communist Party in America had seen a huge rise in membership after the Great Depression, in part because many workers viewed the party as the only political organization that would fight for them.

Betty started meeting with Liz and her husband on her days off. Through them, she met all kinds of fascinating young people. "For us, the big thing was to escape the 'bourgeois' narrow world of our parents, 'the middle class,'" said Betty. But, it was not enough just to be liberal; one had to be radical, even revolutionary.

Betty was so caught up in the political idealism of the era that one day, before she left for Berkeley, she looked up the address of the Communist Party headquarters in New York City and went in to inquire about membership. For whatever reason, she did not follow through with becoming a member.

Betty headed west to Berkeley, California, in September of 1942 at the age of twenty-one. She was enthusiastic about her decision to study at Berkeley, a campus known for its radical, intellectual atmosphere. The trip took two days and two nights aboard the Santa Fe train. She flirted with some of the GIs who were heading off to war, but spent most of the trip overwhelmed with a sense of anxiety as she rehashed her decision to enroll in graduate school. Should she have gone to work in the labor union movement, or even the Communist Party, instead? Maybe she should have pursued a career as a journalist or worked harder at finding a husband, as many of her friends had done.

By the time she arrived in San Francisco, the train's last stop before Berkeley, her anxiety level had risen to such a level, and her asthma was so bad, she needed oxygen and a doctor. Finally, with more apprehension than anticipation, Betty Goldstein entered the gates of the UC Berkeley campus, ready to start her new life as a graduate student.

Betty settled into a residence house called the Red Castle, on Channing Way, where many of the more radical students lived. Many of her professors were leftist radicals or communist supporters, and she loved them right from the start. But she found her psychology classes to be disappointing. Freud's ideas were just beginning to be taught at UC Berkeley, and it seemed the school was somewhat behind her alma mater.

She read her Smith undergraduate thesis to a faculty symposium and they told her it was so good that she could have saved it to use as her graduate thesis or Ph.D. dissertation. The symposium recommended her for the highest science fellowship available at the time, the Abraham Rosenberg Research Fellowship. Betty was somewhat disillusioned by the symposium's assessment, believing it indicated that the university's master's degree program might not be challenging enough. But she attempted to resurrect her enthusiasm for graduate studies through her proposed master's thesis, titled "Critical Review of the Psychoanalytical Theory of Personality Types." In it she planned to apply Gestalt thinking to Freud's concepts of the oral, anal, and genital stages of personality development to see how his theories held up.

Around this same time, Betty met Bob Loevinger, a physicist and protégé of J. Robert Oppenheimer, who was then developing the atomic bomb at Los Alamos, New Mexico. Bob's work in the Berkeley lab was top secret. He never talked about it, other than to say it had to do with the war. Betty later speculated as to her reasons for dating Bob. Most of the boys her age were off to war, Bob was a member of a radical study group, she was in love with the idea of being in love, and "he took [her] to real Chinese restaurants in San Francisco, not like the chop suey ones in Peoria."

That Christmas, Betty went home for vacation. She took a trip to Chicago to use the library at the University of Chicago and to talk with Franz Alexander, one of the leading pioneers in the theory of psychosomatic illness, about her thesis. While in Chicago, she stopped for a visit with her high-school friend Paul Jordan, who was in medical school at the university. When she arrived home, she found that her father's health had deteriorated badly. He was nearly delirious with his illness, and in this fevered state, he accused her of having sex with Paul when she visited him. Furious at his false allegations, she stormed from his room and did not see him again before returning to California.

Back at Berkeley, Betty was called out of class on January 11, 1943, and given the news that her father had died, less than two weeks after she had last seen him. She took her first ever ride in an airplane, and arrived in Peoria in time for his open-casket viewing. She stared long and hard at his grim face and realized the difficult life he had lived. "He seemed an old man, though he was barely sixty, and I suddenly felt this enormous hatred of my mother. I felt the pressures my father must have felt, with his business and Gentile customers and bankers, and the way my mother made him feel so inadequate, so inferior. Why couldn't she give him the love he needed?... I swore again not to be the kind of woman my mother was. But something went dead inside me," she admitted.

Grieving, Betty returned to California where she went through the motions of attending classes and continuing her relationship with Bob. A few months later, in March 1943, Betty learned that she had won the Abraham Rosenberg Research Fellowship. It would pay for her education all the way through a Ph.D. This was the first time a psychologist had won the fellowship and the first time it had ever been awarded to a woman. Instead of feeling elation, however, Betty suffered an asthma attack and a case of anxiety so severe that her body broke out in welts.

Shortly thereafter, Betty and Bob were strolling in the Berkeley hills behind the lab, when Bob told her, "You can take that fellowship, but you know I'll never get one like it. You know what it will do to us." Goldstein could not remember what she said next, but she did remember feeling that "if I took that fellowship, if I went on in this academic world where it was so easy for me to be brighter than the boys, I would never be able to be the kind of woman my mother wasn't [a kind, loving wife and mother]. I lost sight of the possibility that I had sensed even as a child, saying my prayers, that if my mother had a career of her own that made her feel good enough about herself as a woman she might have been better able to love her husband and children."

It isn't fair

—the way the work of the human race is proportioned out and distributed.

Look at the drudgery of washing clothes and cleaning house. Compare it in its hardness and wearingness with the occupations of most men! The only way out of it is to use Pearline.

Use Pearline and take the drudgery away from housework. Pearline makes woman's work womanly and healthful and fit for her to do. All the washing, all the cleaning, and hundreds of other things besides, are made easy with Pearline.

Millions *USE* Pearline

This 1897 advertisement showcases sexist thinking disguised as a kind of feminism. Fifty years later, women were still expected to marry, raise, children, and care for home and family.

Betty decided to give up the fellowship and her graduate studies without consulting any of her professors. She was embarrassed to tell them the real reason, that she was doing it for a man, so she told them she was giving up a career in psychology in order to work for the "revolution," loosely defined as supporting communism, workers' rights, and labor unions. She thought her professors would approve since many of them were for the revolution, as well. She went so far as to contact the editor of *People's World,* the West Coast communist newspaper— a move that she believed skirted the issue of having a career because it involved doing reporting and editorial work for a political cause she believed in.

Betty later described her embrace of Marxism:

> I remember the sharp distinction I had learned in my economics classes at Smith where I studied communism, fascism, capitalism—that fascism was capitalism carried to the extreme, absolute power to those who owned the industries and banks, no freedom of the people to organize or express dissent. No unions allowed to strike against workers' oppression, no social thinkers allowed to be critical of the system…we learned that communism was a system that put the interests of the people first and in which private profit from the exploitation of workers was abolished.

The editor at *People's World* turned down Betty's job application, however. Along with several of her profes-

Betty enjoying a boating excursion while on a camping trip. *(Courtesy of The Schlesinger Library, Radcliffe Institute, Harvard University.)*

sors, he tried to convince her that she would help the revolution far more by becoming a psychology professor. Goldstein was not to be dissuaded. She later wrote, "I never could explain, hardly knew myself, why I gave up th[at] career." She practically had a nervous breakdown and suffered some of her most severe coughing and asthma attacks to date.

In spite of her decision to forgo the fellowship and a career, Betty's relationship with Bob ended. She felt guilt-ridden for having given up her plans, and morally obligated to work either for the war effort or the revolution. Initially, Betty had been opposed to WWII, not because she was a pacifist per se, but because she was anti-fascist and had "learned about the evils of capitalism and how munitions makers profited from war." Like many of her fellow Smith students and *SCAN* editors, Betty had believed that America's entry into the war was not the best way to fight fascism, which was her primary concern. They believed that, rather than diluting democracy by fighting a foreign war with uncertain political results, America should strengthen democracy at home by taking steps such as allowing laborers to unionize. When Japan attacked Pearl Harbor on December 7, 1941, however, Betty changed her position to support America's involvement in the war.

Betty tried to get a job at the Office of War Information in Washington, D.C. after the *People's World* editor turned her down, but her college editorials and communist associations made her too radical for the agency's hiring protocol. She retreated to Peoria for the summer of

1943. Her mother was living at the Jefferson Hotel, having sold the house after Betty's father died. Amy had moved to Boston and Harry Jr. had joined the army. Betty jumped at the chance to join several of her Smith alumnae friends to rent a little house in Greenwich Village in New York City. She was twenty-two and grateful to be leaving Peoria once again. She found a job, not a "career," as a reporter for the *Federated Press*. It was a small left-wing newspaper agency that provided articles to labor, liberal, and radical newspapers around the country.

Goldstein was paid thirty dollars a week, roughly half the salary paid to male reporters, which was not an unusual practice at the time. She loved the work and felt in some respects that she was back at *SCAN*. She covered the first major labor strike over race relations in Philadelphia and wrote articles exposing injustices that were perpetrated against groups of people simply because the victims were Jewish, women, or African American. She recounted the struggles between labor and business, generally lambasting business for its greediness and its efforts to strip labor of any power. She also suffered writer's block, asthma attacks, and continued bouts of anxiety. At times her editor was forced to rip the pages from her typewriter in order to meet a deadline.

Her personal life was a large contributor to her anxiety. She socialized with the *Federated Press* staff regularly, hung out at the bar in the Newspaper Guild building, and maintained two circles of friends outside of work. One circle included communists, socialists, pacifists, African Americans, and working class people who couldn't have fathomed the luxury of her life in Peoria. The other circle included her Smith friends, who visited her in New York regularly. While Betty wanted her wealthier friends' acceptance and friendship, she also sneered at their shallow values, which often centered on the search for a rich husband. Her relations with men were also stressful. According to one co-worker, when it came to men, Betty was extremely insecure and would go to great lengths to prove herself with them.

In an attempt to get a grip on her anxiety, Betty began undergoing psychoanalysis. Her mother had remarried and given each of her children seven thousand dollars, their share of the proceeds from the sale of the Goldstein Jewelry Company. Betty chose to use her portion to deal with the painful memories of her mother and to understand the origins of her respiratory problems, anxiety, and periods of writer's block.

Near the end of World War II, psychological theories and principles and psychoanalysis became widely incorporated into American culture for the first time. Scores of European psychologists, many of whom were Jewish, had fled to America during the war. By the late 1940s and early 1950s, great numbers of Americans were taking advantage of psychoanalysis in hopes of better understanding their own psyches.

By September 1945, when Betty was twenty-four-years old, World War II officially ended and the GIs began to return home. One of them took Betty's job at *Federated Press*—returning veterans were entitled to take back the jobs they had vacated when they left for the war. For the next six years, she worked as a labor journalist for the *UE News,* the official publication of the United Electrical, Radio, and Machine Workers Union of America, one of the more radical labor unions. Early in 1946, for example, it had shut down all of the Westinghouse and General Electric factories in the United States and Canada, which set up a highly adversarial relationship between these corporations and the union.

Betty described her years writing for *UE News* as being in "the vanguard of the working-class revolution." She also continued her participation in Marxist discussion groups and called herself "very political, very involved, consciously radical." Her roommates were starting to get married and, one by one, left the Greenwich Village house. Eventually, no one remained to share the rent so Betty moved to a small, one-bedroom apartment, with no kitchen, located in the basement of a brownstone at Eight West Eighty-sixth Street. She was living entirely alone for the first time in her life, and found it terrifying.

Betty accepted right away when her friend and fellow labor reporter, Fred Zeserson, asked if she wanted to go on a blind date with an old army buddy of his. "He brought me an apple on our first date, and made me laugh," she said of Carl Friedman. Two months later, Carl moved into her apartment.

Carl was born in Chelsea, Massachusetts in 1919. His parents had immigrated from Latvia and did not have the type of success that the Goldsteins' family had experienced. The Friedmans (Carl and Betty would later change

Betty and Carl during the early, happy years of their relationship. *(Courtesy of The Schlesinger Library, Radcliffe Institute, Harvard University.)*

the name to Friedan) lived in slums and moved often when they could not pay the rent. Wherever they lived was usually filled with anger and bitterness. Carl said, "My mother had no love to give. She approved of nothing I did. . . . She and my father screamed at each other continually. She would threaten to kill herself. I never saw my father and mother kiss." His Aunt Polly became something of a surrogate mother to him.

To escape this domestic chaos, Carl spent his free time at vaudeville shows and taught himself to do magic tricks, which he practiced for hours. Eventually, he loaded up his beat-up old Ford and toured New England's vaudeville shows and summer hotels and camps, booking himself as "Carlyn the Magician." He then went to the University of Massachusetts, where he barely scraped by financially. He was described by one college friend as a rebel, very unconventional, and thoroughly unsuccessful at dating. He transferred to Emerson College and studied playwriting, acting, and directing, but did not graduate. He enlisted in the U.S. Army Signal Corps in 1942.

Carl joined Mickey Rooney's Soldiers Show Company, which provided entertainment for the troops. He traveled all over Europe, designing and building the company's sets, and worked with the singer and dancer Danny Kaye. During these war years he drove his own jeep and threw wild parties. He later described the experience as the most carefree time of his life.

Carl and Betty married in a New York City Hall civil ceremony on June 12, 1947, approximately one year after their first date. Betty was convinced she loved him and that they had a lot in common. Carl, on the other hand, later said, "I was lonely in the city, and I moved in. It was comfortable, but it wasn't real love. She had an underlying warmth. She was in analysis. I knew I had a need for it [analysis]. That was an attraction. And just being lonesome."

Betty and Carl followed their simple civil ceremony with a Jewish wedding under a *huppa* (the ceremonial canopy under which the bride and groom stand in typical Jewish weddings), at Carl's insistence. When they returned from their honeymoon, Carl delved into fixing up their basement apartment. His set designing and building experience made him handy at carpentry and he managed to squeeze a cooking area into the tiny apartment. They started giving parties: "we always gave great parties," Betty said, and their lives quickly settled into a routine.

Carl worked as an assistant manager for a theater troupe and Betty continued working for *UE News*. Her articles were as radical as ever. In one, she criticized the AFL and CIO union leaders' agreement to hold wages down during the Korean War. She called for "equality of sacrifice," when she heard that one wealthy "heiress to an armaments fortune bought $6,000 worth of southern resort clothes in one hour in a swanky Fifth Avenue dress-shop." This amount exceeded the annual salary of many American workers.

Betty also railed against discrimination levied against Jews and African Americans. She asked, "[where is] the morality of one bill of rights for people whose skin is

white and another for those with black skin, one kind of
jobs for whites and another for black; streets to live on,
schools, hotels, polling places, places to fish and camp—
open to all Americans who can pay the price or pass the
examination—except to Americans whose skin is black."
She wrote a similar piece about an investigatinon by the
House of Representatives into purported communist influence in Hollywood. In it, she bemoaned the fact that
people who had fled Nazi Germany to gain the freedoms
of speech, association, and expression now faced similar
restrictions in America. It was apparent that marriage
had not changed Betty's opinions nor calmed her radicalism.

Chapter Five

Suburban Housewife and Mother

Betty and Carl returned to Peoria to attend her brother's wedding in the fall of 1947. On their way home, they visited her longtime friends, Harriet Vance and John Parkhurst. The two had married and recently had a baby. Seeing their baby sparked Betty and Carl's decision to have one of their own.

Daniel (Danny) Friedan was born on October 3, 1948. His birth was heralded with an announcement designed by Carl in the form of a theatrical ad. Before Danny's birth, twenty-seven-year-old Betty had immersed herself in preparing for his delivery and care. She was determined to do motherhood differently than her mother had.

UE News granted her one year of maternity leave, of which six weeks were paid, but called her back to the office a couple of months early, in August, to allow other reporters to take vacations. She had no choice, she felt, as Carl did not earn enough money working in the summer theater to take the family through the winter months. The family needed

Betty's salary of one hundred dollars a week.

Betty felt nervous and guilty about leaving her baby to return to work. She had read books on child rearing, including the famous Dr. Spock's *Baby and Child Care,* which, while progressive in some areas, still cautioned mothers that they would damage their children by leaving them to return to jobs. Betty later said how lucky she was to have a pediatrician who opined that, in spite of what Dr. Spock said, her baby would not be damaged by her going back to work.

As she later explained, "At that time in my life, there's no question that motherhood came first, though there was also no question for me that I wasn't committed to my job or that I wouldn't do it well. I made new rules for myself, get in by 10:30 A.M. (the men often came in that late, stopping for breakfast en route), skip lunch if necessary, and get my errands and shopping done, then leave by 5:00. And since by [then] I was a good, fast writer, no one could complain I didn't get my work done."

Nonetheless, Betty was getting frustrated with Carl's lack of a steady income. She started nagging him to get a job in television, a relatively new invention. Carl later confessed that he pretended to look for work every day but was frozen with fear. Betty eventually convinced him to borrow money from his Aunt Polly to go into analysis. Carl said, "A great deal of my analysis was how to deal with Betty." His analyst told him he had married a woman just like his mother, a popular Freudian concept.

About that same time, Betty was growing more and more uneasy about communism. Several inconsistencies

Betty, Carl, and their first child, Daniel, in 1949. *(Courtesy of The Schlesinger Library, Radcliffe Institute, Harvard University.)*

between the communist doctrine and its implementation in the government of the Soviet Union were coming to light. These included the gulag (prison labor camp) atrocities, the non-aggression pact that had been signed between the fascist Hitler and the communist Stalin, and the suppression of dissent. Betty was especially disillusioned with the Marxist concept of labor and economic value in which women's work and the nurturing of the family had no worth.

Several essays she read at the time affected her, especially those included in T.W. Adorno's *The Authoritarian Personality.* Betty said that these essays provided "an elucidation of the conditions and kinds of personality that can turn any revolutionary 'ism' into authoritarian dogma, and stifle the free human spirit and democratic expression necessary for society to evolve." Another influential essay was Hannah Arendt's "On Revolution." Betty said Arendt's groundbreaking work gave her "the insight that, unlike other revolutions, which resulted in overthrow or transfer of power from one group to another, the American Revolution resulted in a structure which continues in perpetuity the *process* of revolution, the democratic process embodied in our Constitution, giving it continued rebirth, the continuing process of questioning, of confronting problems, new challenges, new ideas, reaffirming truths to meet changing conditions."

Several national and worldwide events raised further concerns about communism. These included the Soviet Union's expansion in eastern Europe, China's fall to a communist government, the Soviet Union's explosion of its first atomic bomb, and America's entry into the Korean War to halt the spread of communism.

In 1950 Congress passed the Internal Security Act, which required members of the Communist Party and similar organizations to register with the Department of Justice. Later that same year, U.S. Senator Joseph McCarthy began to use his senatorial committee to launch a public search for anyone he suspected of having communist connections. McCarthy operated from accusations and innuendo. It soon became apparent that his goal was not, as he initially claimed, to root out communists who might be in sensitive positions in the government, but simply to destroy the careers and even lives of anyone he decided was his enemy. McCarthy helped to unleash an anti-communist sentiment that made most Americans, Betty included, want to conform and blend in with everyone else. Betty later explained this phenomenon and her own political shift: "After the loneliness of war and the unspeakableness of the bomb, against the frightening uncertainty, the cold immensity of the changing world, women as well as men sought the comforting reality of home and children."

Danny was now almost three years old and Betty felt he needed other children to play with. While she was looking for a neighborhood they might relocate to, she read an article about a wonderful cooperative nursery school in a community built by the United Nations in Queens, New York. Called Parkway Village, it had been built for UN personnel and was also open to former GIs and newspaper correspondents. Betty and Carl fell in love with this community of intellectually stimulating people from all over the world who almost immediately became one another's extended families. Carl's GI status qualified them for admittance, and Betty was soon decorating their new apartment in wild colors like red and purple with modern, designer furniture—Eames chairs and a free-form, three-corner Noguchi dining table.

Within a year, Betty wanted to have another child. Danny was four and they did not want him to be an only child. When she got pregnant, though, Carl did not react to the news as she had expected. He began making excuses for not coming home, and their arguments about his lack of earnings grew fiercer. Complicating the situation was *UE News*'s decision to fire Betty for no apparent reason. She complained to the Newspaper Guild and was told, "It's your fault for getting pregnant again."

Betty was angry but at the same time a bit relieved about her termination. She had been reading popular books and magazine articles that claimed "career women" undermined their husband's masculinity and stunted their children's growth. She had also recently learned that Carl was having an affair with an old girlfriend. This seemed to support the idea that her working was somehow the problem in their relationship. She accepted her termination without putting up a fight.

One of the last pieces Betty wrote as a labor reporter was a thirty-nine-page pamphlet published in 1952 and titled "UE Fights for Women Workers." In this pamphlet, she identified the contradiction between the electrical manufacturing industry's treatment of women as workers and its treatment of women as consumers. She described how the industry glorified women in domestic roles with advertisements that featured them cooking in their General Electric kitchens, sorting clothes at their Westinghouse washing machines, and lounging in front of their Sylvania television sets. Betty zeroed in on the dichotomy of an industry that sold their products to one group of American women, while the women who made the products could not afford to buy them because their wages were so low.

To that end, Betty advocated that women deserved equal pay for equal work, and that the discriminatory

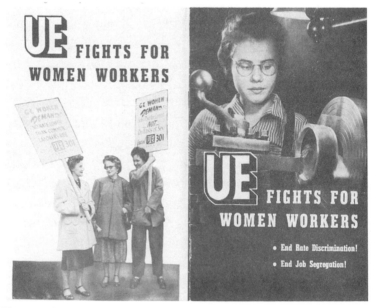

The cover of Betty's 1952 *UE News* pamphlet. *(Courtesy of The Schlesinger Library, Radcliffe Institute, Harvard University.)*

practices that kept women in lower-paying jobs had to be abolished. Further, she argued, men had to support the fight to make these changes.

Meanwhile, Carl was still not making a steady income. Now that he was the family's sole provider, he had to leave the theater entirely. He formed a partnership with Fred Zeserson, his old army buddy, to open a public relations and advertising firm. Betty discovered that she missed working. She decided to return to therapy and was taken aback when her therapist asked her, "Why are you pretending to be just a housewife? Didn't you graduate *summa cum laude* in psychology? Aren't you a writer?" She avoided answering these questions for the time being. Instead, she focused her attention on preparing for the delivery of her second child.

Jonathan was born on November 27, 1952. Soon after, Betty decided that she needed to work, and once again she turned to writing. This time her target market was the mainstream women's magazines—*Glamour, Good Housekeeping, McCall's, Ladies' Home Journal* and *Redbook*. She got an agent, took a class in writing fiction at Queens College, and changed her name to Betty Friedan. The latter move was an attempt to disassociate herself from her prior communist leanings, political activities, and work as a labor journalist. The articles she would write for these mainstream magazines had to meet their editorial policies. This meant articles that related to housewives and their accepted roles as wives and mothers.

Betty Friedan, as she was now known, rationalized her decision to take on a new name and to change her direction. She told herself that the quantity and type of writing she would be doing did not really amount to a career. So, with that reasoning, she was not really doing any harm to her children or husband. She also believed that she had no choice. In addition to her desire to write, her family needed the income.

Friedan was soon writing articles with titles such as "Day Camp in the Driveways" and "The Happy Families of Hickory Hill." She used a portion of her earnings to hire a maid to take over the household chores while she did her research and interviews. Then, she got pregnant again. Their Parkway Village apartment did not seem big enough for a family of five.

Friedan had lately written some articles on a new

One of the articles Betty wrote for *Parents* magazine. *(Courtesy of The Schlesinger Library, Radcliffe Institute, Harvard University.)*

phenomenon—suburbia—with titles such as "To Get a House, They Built a Community." In the fifteen years following World War II, the baby boom (the term that referred to the record numbers of babies born after the war ended) created a shortage of houses for the growing families. The problem was made worse because the Depression and World War II had slowed housing construction nearly to a halt.

More housing had to be built quickly. Because land was both scarce and expensive in cities, the development of suburbs seemed an easy solution to the housing shortage. Suburbs were housing developments built in areas surrounding a city. The developers generally repeated the same handful of floor plans over and over, on street after street, in order to minimize construction time and cost. Paint color, landscaping, and a different orientation of the garage, for instance, were often the only distinguishing features from house to house. This uniformity of construction gave the suburb an eerie feeling of sameness. To help growing families afford a home in the suburbs, the federal government provided low interest loans through the GI Bill for returning soldiers and through the Federal Housing Administration (FHA) for the working class. Though Friedan hated the blandness of suburbia on first sight, she was considering the possibility of leaving the city.

Then, one day, she found an old stone barn for rent along the Hudson River in Sneden's Landing, about an hour's drive from New York City. It was truly a barn, complete with stalls on the first floor, but it had a rustic appeal that charmed her. Friedan wanted more than anything to be a "happy, fulfilled suburban housewife and soon-to-be mother of three" and to forget she had ever been a part of the communist movement that was now virulently opposed by most Americans. To be happy in her roles as wife and mother would make her different from her own mother, who had been so unhappy. Betty clung to the desire to succeed where her mother had so miserably failed. It would also make her like the majority of middle-class American women and hopefully earn her acceptance, something that was equally important to her. Friedan convinced Carl that moving to the suburbs was the answer.

They made the move in 1956. Some of the barn's charm wore off when the first heating bills arrived. They had to charge their groceries in order to have enough cash to cover other expenses. Friedan missed her Parkway Village friends and became almost completely dependent on Carl for adult companionship and support. One afternoon while loading groceries in the supermarket parking lot, she felt a tremendous anxiety, far worse than any asthma attack she had ever experienced. She started to nag Carl about earning more money and getting home in time for dinner. "I seem to remember a sense of unspeakable horror, fear; I felt numb, until, one night, he hit me," she said. Afterward, they both tried hard to carry on as if nothing had happened.

On May 23, 1956, Friedan delivered her third child, a daughter they named Emily. Shortly afterwards, Friedan started writing again. She found a woman to clean the house and watch over her children while she worked. But she slowly realized she could not bear working for her editors. They seemed to have an unshakeable assumption that women could not identify with any article dealing with politics, science, travel, education, nuclear weapons, or even their own communities, unless it was written in terms of a woman's concern for her husband or children.

The costs of keeping up the stone barn convinced Friedan and Carl they needed to find a house of their own, one they could afford to keep warm. They found a large, older home overlooking the Hudson River, six miles north of Sneden's Landing, in a village called Grandview-on-Hudson. It had eleven rooms, including a gorgeous, spacious living room. As poor as they were, Carl and Betty managed to buy the place for $25,000 with a $2,500 down payment because Carl qualified for a GI loan.

Betty set about making new friends, fixing up the house, and participating in an active social life in Grandview-on-Hudson. She joined the Parent Teacher Association (PTA) and formed carpools with other mothers to take the children to after-school activities. She and Carl both spent a great deal of time with their children, Carl more so on the weekends. Betty loved reading to them and discussing how things worked. Soon, she and Carl were throwing frequent parties, which rapidly became infamous. One neighbor recalled their house as always open, always fun, lively, and welcoming.

With three children and a home in the suburbs, Friedan

The rambling old Victorian Betty and Carl purchased in Grandview-on-Hudson. *(Courtesy of The Schlesinger Library, Radcliffe Institute, Harvard University.)*

tried to convince herself that she was content and fulfilled. Former presidential candidate Adlai Stevenson had defined America's view of the ideal American woman when he gave the commencement address to the Smith College class of 1955. "Women," he said, "have a unique opportunity to influence us, man and boy . . . to inspire in her home a vision of the meaning of life and freedom . . . to help her husband find values that will give purpose to his specialized daily chores . . . to teach her children the uniqueness of each individual human being. . . . This assignment for you, as wives and mothers, you can do in the living room with a baby on your lap or in the kitchen with a can opener in your hand. . . . I think there is much you can do . . . in the humble role of housewife. I would wish you no better vocation than that."

Friedan tried to immerse herself in that role. But she was still compelled, for both economic reasons and her own satisfaction, to continue writing. She joined the Society of Magazine Writers and enrolled in a workshop to train as a professional television writer. Once again, she was felled by severe asthma attacks when she was forced to skip her duties as den mother for Danny's Cub Scout meetings in order to attend the workshops. When she tried to skip the workshops in order to stay with the Scout meetings, she suffered more asthma attacks. She decided in favor of her duties as den mother, saying, "It was more important to be a good mother and stick with Cub Scout meetings, wasn't it?"

What she found herself doing instead of writing was spending more time on school board politics, community activities, PTA work, neighborhood events, bake sales, the League of Women Voters, and the Women's Division of the Democratic Party. Friedan believed there was only so much a mother could do for her children, her husband, and her home; the rest of the time had to be filled with something else. The question for her was, with what?

Friedan decided to do a questionnaire for her Smith College Class of 1942's fifteenth reunion, which was coming up in 1957. She wanted to test the assumption put forth in the hugely popular book *Modern Women: The Lost Sex*. The authors had declared that what was wrong with American women was too much education because it kept them from being good housewives and mothers. Friedan planned to use her findings as the basis for an article she pitched to *McCall's* magazine tentatively titled "Are Women Wasting Their Time in College?"

Friedan and two friends worked on the questionnaire. Her degree in psychology and her years of magazine research and interviewing experience helped them immeasurably. They grouped the questions into subjects: Marriage, Children, Home, Finances, Sex Life, The Other Part (i.e., Did you have ambitions?), Intellectual, Political, Religious, Social, and Personal. Two hundred alumnae responded.

When Friedan presented the findings at the June 1957 alumnae gathering, she reported that 89% of the respondents described themselves as housewives; 60% of those said they did not feel fulfilled; and 80% said their greatest regret was not planning to link their education to a profession. Friedan decided to interview the Smith seniors graduating in the class of 1957. She was alarmed to learn that they were even more committed to the notion that their sole vocation was to be a good housewife and mother.

Friedan's article concluded that it was not going to college and earning a higher education that caused women's frustration. Rather, it was the narrowly defined role of a successful woman as wife and mother. *McCall's* refused to publish the article. Friedan was shocked. She had never had an article turned down. Her agent submitted the article to *Ladies' Home Journal,* which tried to rewrite it, but Friedan refused to accept their changes. *Redbook* magazine responded to her agent's submission: "Betty has always done good work for us before. But she must be going off her rocker. Only the most neurotic housewife will identify with this."

Every time her article was turned down, Friedan did more research and broadened her interview base to include doctors, counselors, and other housewives. She became more convinced than ever that she was onto something, an intuitive response to what she called her inner Geiger counter—the sensation she got when she heard something that was not quite right.

One morning in April 1959, Friedan's inner Geiger counter went off again while she eavesdropped on a conversation that five suburban mothers were having over coffee. She overhead the desperation in one woman's voice as she quietly spoke of her problems. In that moment, Friedan sensed that all of them, herself and her fellow Smith alumnae included, seemed to share the same problem: "I'm Jim's wife, and Janey's mother, a putter on of diapers and snowsuits, a server of meals, a Little League chauffeur. But who am I, as a person myself? It's like the world is going on without me."

Suddenly, Friedan knew why no major woman's magazine would ever publish her article—its claims threatened their very existence. Those highly profitable magazines defined a woman's world that revolved almost entirely around a woman's role as housewife and mother. Friedan knew that the only way her article would be published was if she expanded it into a book. She began querying book publishers and, in 1958, George Brockway at Norton Publishing Company gave her a $3,000 advance to write it. She had a year to finish the book. She was thirty-seven years old.

Chapter Six

Launching a Revolution

Friedan wrote the first two chapters of her book in the Frederick Lewis Allen Room at the New York City Public Library. She used her old typewriter. Three or four days a week she would take the train into the city after dropping Emily off at nursery school. It was a terribly slow process. The more she learned, the more questions she had and the more research she had to do.

When all three of her children were in school and she had more uninterrupted time, Friedan took her boxes of notes and research materials home to Grandview. Her publisher had liked her first two chapters, but Friedan felt something was missing. Anxiety was taking hold as she started to doubt her ability to finish the book.

Then, one night, after putting her children to bed—Carl was staying late at the office, again—she sat down on the couch with a pad of yellow paper and let her mind wander. She thought about her decision to turn down the fellowship that would have allowed her to get her Ph.D.

She remembered the panic she had felt that spring afternoon in 1942 when she had no vision of a future after Smith College. She remembered her guilt about wanting to write in addition to being a housewife and mother. She contemplated the hundreds of women she had interviewed who had similar experiences. The words started to flow as she wrote in longhand the third and crucial chapter of her book, "The Crisis in Woman's Identity." The dam had broken.

It was in 1963, five years after she had signed the contract, that *The Feminine Mystique* was published. Its opening paragraph reads:

> The problem lay buried, unspoken, for many years in the minds of American women. It was a strange

Betty and her two boys. *(Courtesy of The Schlesinger Library, Radcliffe Institute, Harvard University.)*

stirring, a sense of dissatisfaction, a yearning that women suffered in the middle of the twentieth century in the United States. Each suburban wife struggled with it alone. As she made beds, shopped for groceries, matched slipcover material, ate peanut butter sandwiches with her children, chauffeured Cub Scouts and Brownies, lay beside her husband at night—she was afraid to ask even of herself the silent question—'Is this all?'

Friedan dubbed the "problem" she referred to as the "feminine mystique." It was the widely accepted notion that the only fulfillment a woman could have was in her role as housewife and mother, and that careers, higher education, political rights, independence, and opportunities conflicted with that fulfillment. Additionally, Friedan argued that it was American institutions, laws, and social values that had pressured women to confine themselves to family and home. For example, in all of 1963 and 1964, only seventeen women had graduated from the nation's dental schools because of admissions restrictions that favored men. Stewardesses were required to resign when they got married, pregnant, or turned thirty. As well, women who were pregnant or wanted to return to their jobs after giving birth were fired, and women who were raped had to have an eye-witness willing to testify on their behalf before they could file charges.

Friedan ended her book with the chapter "A New Life Plan for Women," which suggested that women should use their lives and abilities as men did in order to balance the demands of family and career. Women should not have to choose between children and work any more than men should.

The book hit a nerve with many Americans. Copies of *The Feminine Mystique* flew off the shelves. *McCall's, Ladies' Home Journal,* and *Mademoiselle* all published excerpts, and within the first year, three hundred thousand copies of the book sold. The book was translated into thirteen languages and sold around the world. Friedan had touched women like no other author before. Her book was deeply personal and had an incredible sense of urgency. Her keenly expressed psychological insights gave voice to feelings the readers had been unable to communicate themselves. The book also gave women reason to ponder the idea of changing their lives. Suddenly, women realized they were not alone, nor were they somehow deficient or outrageous for questioning the roles that had been laid out for them.

The Feminine Mystique launched a revolutionary change in people's consciousness. Friedan's new agent arranged lecture and book-signing tours across the country. She appeared on television talk shows and was featured in *Life* magazine. She was an overnight celebrity. The success of *The Feminine Mystique* prompted Random House to offer Friedan a $30,000 advance to write her next book, tentatively titled "The New Woman."

Though Friedan was experiencing tremendous success in her public life, her private life was falling apart. Both she and Carl were drinking too much and they fought frequently. Carl was becoming known as Mr.

WHAT KIND OF WOMAN ARE YOU?

FRANTIC COOK?

Chauffeur?

Smothered
Mother?

TOO INVOLVED?

Restless?

Interesting?

Informed?

Responsible
Parent?

Motivated?

Satisfied?

BETTY FRIEDAN
author, "THE FEMININE MYSTIQUE"

Betty Friedan will help you decide when she speaks on

 "A NEW IMAGE OF WOMAN"

Attend Temple Emanu-El Sisterhood

DONOR LUNCHEON

Tuesday, October 29, 1963

Sherry - 11:30 a.m.   Luncheon - 12:15 p.m.

Betty promoted her book by meeting and speaking with women all over the country.
(Courtesy of The Schlesinger Library, Radcliffe Institute, Harvard University.)

Betty Friedan and he deeply resented it. Their relationship became more violent. Physical confrontations were common. But Friedan refused to consider divorce. No one in her family had ever been divorced and she equated it with failure. Besides, she liked being married.

In the spring of 1964, Betty and Carl decided to leave Grandview and move back to New York City. They bought an apartment in the Dakota, at Central Park West and Seventy-second, located in the center of the city's nightlife. There, they threw huge parties that were often attended by celebrities. They now had a full-time maid who also did all of the cooking. They spent huge amounts of money on food and alcohol, which led to serious cash-flow problems.

Prior to the Friedans' return to New York City, President John F. Kennedy had appointed a National Commission on the Status of Women. The Commission had issued its findings in 1963 in a report titled *American Women*. The report detailed the discriminatory wages women earned—usually half of what the average man earned—and the declining numbers of women in professional and executive positions. It gave several recommendations to correct these conditions, including putting an end to sex discrimination for government jobs, requiring paid maternity leave, and aranging for quality child care centers and other services to help working mothers. President Kennedy had subsequently issued an Executive Order to extend this Commission and to create similar commissions in each state. Friedan started attending some of their meetings.

In 1964, Friedan read about the passage of a new law, Title VII of the Civil Rights Act. Title VII banned racial and sexual discrimination in the workplace. As it turned out, the provision concerning sex-based discrimination had been included as a joke. Congressman Howard Smith, a fanatical racial segregationist from Virginia, wanted to kill the Civil Rights Bill. He thought that if he attached an amendment to the bill that also banned sex discrimination his fellow Congressmen would vote against the entire bill. But Representative Martha Griffiths of Michigan, one of a handful of female members of the House of Representatives, demanded a roll call vote. In the Senate, Margaret Chase Smith of Maine, the only woman senator, demanded the same. None of the male senators and representatives wanted to go on record as being opposed to banning sex discrimination. The law passed, but was still treated as a joke. When the chairman of the Equal Employment Opportunity Commission (EEOC), the federal agency charged with overseeing the enforcement of Title VII, was asked at a 1965 press conference what he planned to do about sex discrimination, he replied, "Oh, sex discrimination? I guess we'll have to insist that boys can be Playboy bunnies."

Shortly after learning about Title VII, Friedan read an article in the *New York Times* about a Yale Law School professor named Pauli Murray who had been a keynote speaker at the convention of the General Federation of Women's Clubs. Murray told the group that unless women were prepared to march on Washington, D.C. to demand their civil rights as African Americans were doing, the

Betty and her daughter Emily in 1965. Friedan loved being a mother and she loved her work. *(Courtesy of The Schlesinger Library, Radcliffe Institute, Harvard University.)*

sex provision of Title VII would never be enforced.

Friedan's inner Geiger counter went off again. She looked up Pauli Murray and scheduled a meeting with her that would send Friedan "down the road that would lead to the women's movement." Murray told Friedan about the efforts to bury the Commission's *American Woman* report. She introduced Friedan to Mary Eastwood, who worked for the Office of Legal Counsel in the Department of Justice; Catherine East, who was the

Executive Secretary of the Commission on the Status of Women; and Marguerite Rawalt, a lawyer who headed a task force for the Commission. These women and others became Friedan's underground.

With help from the U.S. Labor Department, they had done all of the staff work for the National Commission on the Status of Women. They had been fighting ever since to keep the Commission's findings from being buried, but feared that going public with their fight would mean they would lose their jobs. These women wanted Friedan to be their voice. She had the notoriety that would draw attention and the freedom to speak her mind without fear of losing her job.

Friedan's first move was to spend time at the EEOC office. One day, she was pulled into the office of Sunny Pressman, an EEOC lawyer, who quickly shut her office door and nervously said, "Nobody ever appointed me to represent women and I'm not a feminist, but I can't stand what's going on here. It's like some secret order has been given not to do battle on the sex discrimination part of Title VII. We're getting hundreds, thousands of complaints, but nobody is supposed to do anything about them. You've got to expose it." Friedan and her underground soon learned that over 50,000 complaints from women that alleged sex discrimination had not been investigated by the EEOC.

For several months, Friedan and her underground worked together with Richard Graham, one of the members of the EEOC, to change the situation. Graham had tried rallying women's groups into applying pressure on

Save his life...
and find your own
BE A NURSE

The field of nursing was marketed to and dominated by women, in part because it involved caregiving, which was considered an acceptable career for a woman.

President Johnson to force the EEOC to stand behind Title VII. Graham had tried to get the EEOC to hear a complaint filed by the thousands of stewardesses forced to resign for getting married, becoming pregnant, and/or turning thirty. He had also tried to get the EEOC to enforce the law that made it illegal to run discriminatory "Help Wanted" ads, such as those that listed a job as being open exclusively to men or exclusively to women. So far, he had not had any success.

The climate against enforcing sex discrimination laws was slowly changing. When the third annual conference of the State Commissions on the Status of Women convened in Washington, D.C., in June of 1966, *The Feminine Mystique* had sold over three million copies. But nothing had yet been done by the EEOC to address the 50,000 complaints. Additionally, the cost of living, particularly the price of homes, had risen dramatically over the last decade. This made it difficult for many working class families to make ends meet on just one income. These wives and mothers had no choice but to enter the workplace. At the same time, the number of middle-class women who could afford to stay home but wanted a career beyond their domestic roles was also growing. This created a large and growing population of women who had experienced sex-based discrimination.

At the third annual conference of the State Commissions on the Status of Women, Friedan invited a dozen or so of the attendees to meet in her hotel room and discuss ways they could make the EEOC enforce Title VII. Some of the women in on the discussion included Kay Clarenbach of the Women's Bureau; Catherine Conroy of the Communications Workers of America; Dorothy Heaner of the United Auto Workers Union (UAW); Muriel Fox, a public relations expert; Caroline Davis from the UAW; Catherine East; Mary Eastwood; and Pauli Murray. They decided to submit a resolution at the conference, but when Kay Clarenbach rose to introduce the resolution it was ruled out of order.

Furious at their treatment, Friedan and twenty-eight attendees arranged to meet a few weeks later, on June 30, 1966. On this momentous day, the women laid "the groundwork for one of the most profound social revolutions of the century"—the founding of the National Organization for Women (NOW). The word "for" rather than "of" was used at Friedan's insistence, to make it clear that men were welcome, too.

NOW officially organized in October 1966 with three hundred charter members. The first meeting was held in the *Washington Post* building in Washington, D.C. The thirty men and women present launched what became known as the second wave of the women's rights movement.

Participants and members of this second wave would become known as feminists and were people who believed in the need to legally and constitutionally secure rights and opportunities for women equal to those of men. The first wave of the women's rights movement had lasted from roughly 1848 through 1950, under the leadership of Elizabeth Cady Stanton, Susan B. Anthony, and others, and had resulted in the ratification of the Nineteenth Amendment, granting women the right to vote.

These first-wave activists were primarily known as suffragists, although they had identified similar problems and fought for many of the same rights as the second-wave feminists now pursued. The second-wave feminists employed many of the same nonviolent political, legal, and social tactics used by participants in the Civil Rights Movement during the 1950s and 1960s.

Betty Friedan was named NOW's first president, Kay Clarenbach Chairman of the Board, and Richard Graham, who had fought so hard for women as a member of the EEOC, was named vice-president. They drafted NOW's first statement of purpose to read: "to take the actions needed to bring women into the mainstream of American society, now, full equality for women, in fully equal partnership with men." It was to be a grassroots movement. Dues were set at five dollars and there were to be no major donors or fundraising events.

The NOW leadership called for an end to job discrimination for women, an end to caps on the number of women admitted into graduate schools, an end to the mass media's harmful stereotypes of women, and an end to policies that claimed to be protective but actually denied women equal job opportunities. There were all kinds of protective policies in the workplace that applied to women only. One such policy prohibited women from lifting more than twenty-five pounds, while placing no such restriction on men. This regulation, in a sense, discriminated against both men and women by suggesting that women are inherently weak and men inherently strong.

As it turned out, Betty Friedan was the right leader at the right time for the fledgling movement. She seemed to have a sixth sense for what the media needed in order to develop stories, and she gave them what they needed with dramatic flair. Friedan described her strategy. "We may only have had six women at a press conference and not many more at our first national action, but we knew we were speaking for 600,000 or 6,000,000 and we acted accordingly and made our point," she said. One of her colleagues described Friedan's style:

> She sweeps through meetings, telephone calls, dinners and speeches with frantic bursts of energy as if each day might be her last. Everything is in motion, not just her words, which come so fast she seems to ignore the necessity of breathing. Her hands gesticulate, wave, flail. Her eyes are deep, dark, charged, and violent as her language. Her nose is long, her hair, despite patient attention at the beauty parlor, often askew. Nothing fits the accepted model of beauty. Yet she exerts a powerful, haunting attractiveness—that special combustion that lights up a few rare individuals interacting with their audience.

NOW held its first official board meeting in 1967. In it, task forces were appointed to deal with the problems women faced in employment, education, religion, poverty, law, politics, and their image in the media. Committees were organized to handle finance, membership, public relations, legislation, and legal activities. Friedan felt that monetary compensation and respect for domestic and volunteer work done by women should also be an issue. Issues such as pregnancy and birth control, maternity leave, child-care, and an equal sharing of the responsibility for children by both parents had to be addressed.

It would also be necessary to pass the Equal Rights Amendment (ERA) to the U. S. Constitution if women were ever to have an equal place in the workforce. Alice Paul, who was one of the key leaders in the suffrage battles that had resulted in the passage of the Nineteenth Amendment, had written the ERA in 1921. When first introduced in Congress in 1923, the ERA read, "Men and women shall have equal rights throughout the United States and every place subject to its jurisdiction." The early supporters of the amendment were members of the National Woman's Party (NWP) founded by Alice Paul. The objective of these early ERA supporters was to eliminate the many inequalities that women still faced after having won the right to vote, such as being excluded from serving on juries or in political office.

Most NOW members thought that taking positions on issues like the ERA and birth control would be moving too fast, too soon. Many labor unions still opposed the ERA, and female union members did not feel they could go against their own unions. Birth control was rarely discussed in private, let alone in public, and the Catholic Church, a number of whose members were in favor of the women's movement, opposed birth control outright. Most NOW members felt that for the group to take positions on issues like the ERA and birth control at this stage would be suicide. Nonetheless, Friedan put these ideas on the table.

By the second National Conference in Washington, D.C., in 1967, NOW's membership had risen to twelve hundred. Much to Friedan's delight, the delegates agreed to support the ERA and women's rights to birth control and abortion. "I felt gooseflesh, I felt that we were accepting the torch from the early fighters and passing it on," she said. But her victory had a price. Those who opposed abortion rights broke away to form WEAL, the Women's Equity Action League, in 1968. Similar and diverse groups would continue to form as the women's movement grew and its participants rallied behind their personal causes.

The public's awareness of NOW and the modern women's movement increased significantly the following year, after Friedan and some other women were denied entrance to the Biltmore Hotel Men's Bar and Grill. They were guests of the hotel attending a NOW board meeting. They were emboldened to protest against their exclusion and agreed "to hold a national day of action against sex discrimination in public accommodations" scheduled for Susan B. Anthony's birthday, February 15. Their idea spread across the country like wildfire.

By the end of 1969, NOW's efforts under Friedan's leadership had resulted in several successes. NOW had supported the flight attendants' lawsuit that had resulted in the EEOC's ruling that airlines could not discriminate based on gender, age, or marital status. NOW had documented sexism in children's textbooks, storybooks, and television programs, so that parents and teachers might better understand the stereotypical roles being portrayed to young boys and girls. The organization had supported the class action sex-discrimination case against the telephone company Southern Bell, which had ended in a victory for female employees. It had also supported federally financed child-care centers, making it possible for many mothers to go to work.

In spite of these huge strides, women could still be dismissed from sitting on juries and fired from their jobs if they became pregnant. It was still legal to discriminate against women when it came to the sale, rental, or financing of housing. There were no laws against sexual harassment in the workplace, nor were women integrated in the U.S. Armed Services or NASA's space program. There were no after-school, high-school, or college sports programs for girls, and the average woman's wage was still roughly half the average man's.

Friedan later wrote of her early years with NOW: "it's been with breathless incredulity that we, ordinary American women—suburban housewives, League of Women Voters volunteers, nuns, trade union members, guilty career women, back-to-school community college students and educators, frustrated women government bureaucrats—started a revolution that transformed society. And as I look back now, tracing small parts that became greater than the whole, I still feel in awe."

In 1969, Friedan worked with activist Larry Lader and others to co-found the National Association for the Repeal of Abortion Laws (NARAL). (NARAL later changed its name to the National Abortion Rights Action League after the Supreme Court's *Roe v. Wade* decision, making abortion legally available to women in the United States.) NARAL's goals were to make it legal for women to have safe abortions during the first term of pregnancy and to make it possible for women to access safe, effective contraception and quality reproductive health care. These were bold concepts in 1969. Estimates of the annual number of illegal abortions obtained by American women during the 1950s and 1960s range from two hundred thousand to 1.2 million. Many states and local governments had laws restricting a single woman's access to birth control. In fact, many states had similar legislation restricting a married woman's access to contraceptive information until a 1965 Supreme Court decision had ruled the practice illegal. Friedan was adamant that she was not pro-abortion. She declared that would be like saying she was pro-mastectomy. Rather, she said, "I am for the *choice to have children.*"

Chapter Seven

Defeats and Victories

The co-founding of NARAL in 1969 proved to be another triumph for Friedan in her ongoing fight for women's rights, but the year also marked what she considered her biggest personal failure. That year she divorced Carl after twenty-two years of marriage. The fighting and physical violence between them had escalated. She felt hypocritical for staying in a violent relationship while she was urging other women to take charge of their own lives. Yet, thirty-one years later, Friedan would say that divorcing Carl was the hardest thing she had ever done.

The following year, 1970, brought even more upheaval in her life. She found herself at odds with various factions and leaders of the women's rights movement, both inside and outside NOW. Some of the younger women joining the movement were more radical in their views. One such group was known as SCUM, the "Society for Cutting Up Men." Others supported "female chauvinism"—the idea that men should be considered second-class citizens. Additionally, sexual politics, particularly protecting the rights of lesbians, was becoming an issue. Friedan believed one's sexuality was a private matter; others believed that lesbian rights should become part of the NOW platform. Perhaps what put Friedan most at odds with her fellow feminists and movement leaders was her leadership style. As one fellow NOW member said, "Betty's greatest strength—her aggressiveness—is also her greatest weakness."

Friedan resigned as the president of NOW in April 1970 at the age of forty-nine to avoid going through a challenge that she might lose. Membership under her leadership had reached three thousand. She gave a two-hour farewell speech and ended by saying, "I have led you into history. I leave you now—to make new history." She called for a massive women's rights demonstration and a twenty-four-hour strike for equality to take place four months later on August 26, 1970, the fiftieth anniversary of the ratification of the Nineteenth Amendment. The new NOW leadership made it clear that Friedan was on her own to organize the strike.

Friedan delved into building a broad coalition of women and men to help with arranging the event—publicity experts, march organizers, and grassroots volunteers. She asked her friends to host benefits and then asked those who attended to host their own. In the end, Friedan agreed to forgo the twenty-four-hour strike for equality as counterproductive but wanted a demonstration to occur in New York City and in NOW chapters across the country.

On August 26, the day of the event, Friedan found herself forced to take a bus uptown and then walk to Fifty-ninth Street because she could not find an available cab. As she rounded the corner into Central Park, she pulled up short. Thousands of women, children, and men, had gathered and many started chanting, "Bet-ty, Bet-ty," when they saw her. A number of New York City's mounted police tried to keep the protestors on the sidewalk but the number of people made crowd control difficult. Friedan surveyed the scene and concluded there was no way they would stay in an orderly line. She waved her arms over her head and rallied the crowd, shouting for them to take the street.

Immediately, somewhere between thirty and fifty thousand demonstrators swarmed onto Fifth Avenue to march for women's rights. Friedan was lodged in the front row between Judge Dorothy Kenyon, a former suffragist now in her eighties, and a member of the new generation of feminists. People shouted their support from office windows along the way and others joined the march en route.

An estimated one hundred thousand more people held similar marches and demonstrations in some ninety cities and small towns across forty-two states. It was a historic day and NOW's membership soared to fifteen thousand. When Congress convened the following January, a record-breaking fourteen women were members.

Friedan and two other well-known feminist leaders, Gloria Steinem and Bella Abzug, believed it was imperative that women now take to the political arena. Women made up approximately fifty-three percent of the population but less than three percent of Congress—only four-teen out of the five hundred thirty-five members were women. Friedan, Steinem, and Abzug knew that women, whether young or old, Republican or Democrat, needed to get involved in all levels of government.

Gloria Steinem was a financially independent, well-known lecturer and journalist, unmarried and without children, who co-founded and edited *Ms.* magazine in 1971. Bella Abzug was a peace activist opposed to the Vietnam War, a lawyer, and a newly elected congress-woman. She had a supportive husband who "did every-thing and anything to make possible what I was doing," she said. Early on, Steinem and Abzug had clicked and worked well together. However, they often found them-selves at odds with Friedan and her leadership style.

There was tension between Friedan and the thirty-seven-year-old Steinem, which made collaboration on their new venture difficult. Steinem was very popular with the younger women in the movement. Liberated by access to the birth control pill, these younger women were entering the workforce and staying, some electing to marry and others not to, some electing to have children and others to remain childless. These were choices that had not been available to women just a decade earlier. Steinem was their role model. These younger women admired her style, single status, financial independence, and achievements.

Steinem, Abzug, and Friedan met in June 1971 for an initial planning session. Their numbers expanded to two thousand, some of whom were congresswomen or active leaders in the Democratic and Republican parties, for an organizing conference held a month later. The group adopted two primary objectives: to get women elected at all levels of government, and to get the major political parties to include passage of the ERA, national child care, and abortion rights to their party platforms. Their slogan was "Make policy, not coffee," and they named the organization the National Women's Political Caucus (NWPC). Gloria Steinem was chosen as NWPC's spokesperson.

Friedan was angered the group selected Steinem instead of her. She was convinced that Abzug had something to do with it, but one of Friedan's NOW allies explained the decision. "People didn't want Betty for two reasons. When Betty talks, she has a tendency to ramble—she can't cut to the gist of it without walking around it twice. The media want[ed] sound bites. And Betty had her own agenda, and nobody knew what it was." Steinem added, "People didn't trust her to speak for the group. She always spoke for herself."

Additionally, it seemed apparent, the media wanted Steinem as well. She would soon appear on the cover of *Newsweek* and be named Woman of the Year by *McCall's*. The latter was particularly galling to Friedan for two reasons. Steinem had not written a book, started an organization, or traveled the country for years speaking and lecturing about women's rights the way Friedan had. Secondly, Friedan was in the process of writing a column for *McCall's* called "Betty Friedan's Notebook" in which she explained the various aspects of the women's movement. Its readership numbered some eight million people. She did not understand how *McCall's* could possibly choose Steinem over herself as Woman of the Year.

Subsequent actions by all three women would deepen the rift developing between them. Friedan wrote an article for the *New York Times Magazine,* "Up From the Kitchen Floor." In it, she took credit for most of the accomplishments of the movement and ranted against lesbians, "man-haters," and members of the extremist feminist groups for taking over and distorting "her" movement. Friedan's secretary said, "It was a huge battle about what she should or shouldn't put in [the article]. I told her she was alienating people and creating political difficulties in the movement. She didn't care. She felt very hurt about not being honored sufficiently. Gloria was taking center stage."

In spite of the acrimony, the NWPC, Friedan, Abzug, and Steinem had more than enough work to do. Congress had finally passed the ERA in 1972, which by then read, "Equality of rights under the law shall not be denied or abridged by the United States or by any State on account of sex." Thirty-eight states had to ratify the ERA before it could become an Amendment to the Constitution of the United States.

ERA supporters thought its ratification was critical in order to provide guidance to the Supreme Court in making future decisions about sex-related discrimination issues. Almost immediately, anti-ERA groups formed, including the Eagle Forum, the Catholic Church's National Right to Life Committee, the John Birch Society, the

Christian Crusade, and the American Education Lobby.

Phyllis Schlafly, leader of the Eagle Forum, emerged as a prominent anti-ERA spokesperson. She was the antithesis of Betty Friedan—tall, immaculately groomed, and willing to play stereotypical female roles. One of Schlafly and the Eagle Forum's signature moves was to give legislators baked breads and homemade jams with notes reading, "To the breadwinners from the bread makers." Friedan found what she called Schlafly's hypocrisy galling. Schlafly had received her law degree at the age of fifty. This would have been impossible without the changes created by women's groups. Schlafly charged and received generous fees for her lectures, wrote professionally, had a biweekly commentary on CBS radio, but nevertheless urged all women to stay home and be satisfied with their roles as wives and mothers. Friedan was incensed at Schlafly's double standards.

Collectively, the anti-ERA groups succeeded in their efforts to distort what the ERA was about and the changes it would bring to American society. The opposition groups claimed it would make wives legally responsible to provide half of their family's financial support, force women to be drafted into the armed forces, force unisex bathrooms, and generally bring about the destruction of motherhood and the family. One of the most egregious charges was that the ERA would make it unconstitutional to have laws that protected women from rape and sexual harassment.

About this same time, far more radical feminist groups, like Redstockings, WITCH, and Cell 16, brought negative publicity to the women's movement. The debate as to whether lesbian rights should be added to the NOW platform was also heating up. The women's movement began to create fissures as these different factions came into conflict. The media sensed the shift in support and stories began to appear characterizing feminists as man-haters and lesbians.

Besieged by money problems and hurt by the continued marginalization of her role in the movement, Betty decided to remove herself from organizational battles and turn her energies to teaching, lecturing, writing, and serving as a sort of international emissary for the women's movement. She toured and spoke about feminism, NOW, the ERA, abortion rights, and women's political power in Brazil, Colombia, Spain, France, and Israel. She visited the Shah and Empress of Iran and secured an audience with Pope Paul VI. This was of particular importance as it demonstrated the international regard in which Betty was held, especially considering the pope's objections to some of the positions Betty espoused.

Pope Paul VI had set up a commission in 1973 to look at the position of women in society and the Church. Several outspoken nuns and priests had been appointed to the commission. The idea for Betty to meet with the pope had come from her good friend Father Francis Xavier Murphy, who was covering the Vatican Council II for *The New Yorker* magazine under his pen name, Xavier Rynne. Friedan and Father Murphy had enjoyed "countless discussions about the church and women."

Father Murphy had set up introductions for Friedan, to

coincide with her visit to Rome in 1973, in an effort to arrange a papal audience. Friedan had no expectations but filled out the application anyway. She was surprised when the meeting was granted. It seemed the pope wanted to talk with her about his commission.

Friedan immediately began preparations; the fuss surrounding the need to cover her head in the presence of the pope was particularly telling. Wearing a hat was considered a sign of submission by the women's movement but was required by the Catholic faith. The famous hatter, Mister John, saved the day by designing a little halo that stood above Freidan's hair, attached by bobby pins—it covered her head, but did not touch her hair.

Apprehension filled Friedan as she recalled Biblical quotations on her walk through the Vatican courtyard: "'Sin began with a woman, and thanks to her, all must die,' from Ecclesiastics; 'Every woman ought to be overcome with shame at the thought that she is a woman,' from St. Clement." But she was immediately at ease in Pope Paul VI's presence.

Friedan presented Pope Paul VI with a symbol of the women's movement—the biological sign for female superimposed over an equal sign that looked a little like a cross. She said, "I bring you this with the wishes of the women of America that the church which has at times been oppressive of women might now become a force for the liberation of women. As you can see from this symbol, when women are completely equal to men, it becomes a different kind of cross." Pope Paul VI presented Friedan with a jewel box that held a medal of his like-

Betty Friedan's historic meeting with Pope Paul VI in 1973. *(Courtesy of The Schlesinger Library, Radcliffe Institute, Harvard University.)*

ness. Friedan reported that they talked about his commission and that he expressed his personal distress over the case of several Portuguese women recently arrested for expressing their feminist beliefs. "He took my hands in his to convey his concern for women and I was as touched as I was heartened," she said.

Emily Friedan had accompanied her mother on many overseas trips since her parents' divorce, but she did not join Betty when she visited the pope. She said of her teen years living with Friedan, "It didn't matter that she was Betty Friedan or a feminist. What came into play was the immense amount of self-involvement it takes to change the world."

Emily entered Radcliffe College in 1973. Friedan sold her personal papers to the school's library in order to pay Emily's tuition. With the last of her children now out of the house, Friedan decided to move into an apartment at 1 Lincoln Plaza, overlooking Central Park and Lincoln Center. She also started what became a ten-year affair with a married man, David Manning White.

White and Friedan had met while leading a workshop designed by National Training Laboratories that used Gestalt principles to teach group leadership techniques. White was a mass communications expert who taught at Boston University. Friedan and White shared an immediate mutual attraction, and when he came to visit her in New York shortly after the workshop ended, they started an affair. White's wife of twenty-five years, Catherine, a biochemist, came to accept the situation. "I couldn't fulfill all of David's needs any more than he could fulfill mine. . . . They [David and Betty] were very much alike. He would set the mood for the whole house. I was glad when he took a week or a weekend off," she said later. White remained devoted to his wife and their sons, as well as to Friedan, whose traveling and lecture schedule suited this arrangement.

Friedan was thrilled to be in love again, and she blossomed under White's attention. They had a very public relationship. He was her escort on many trips and accompanied her to President Jimmy Carter's inauguration ceremony. Later, when she looked back on their affair, she said she could see that she used it as a way to avoid both being alone and getting married again.

Betty and David White. *(Courtesy of The Schlesinger Library, Radcliffe Institute, Harvard University.)*

Friedan's good mood at the time was also enhanced by the growing appreciation for and numerous successes of the women's movement since *The Feminine Mystique*'s publication. NOW chapters existed in some seven hundred U.S. cities and over twenty countries throughout the world. The United Nations had granted NOW non-governmental organization (NGO) status and designated 1975 as the Year of the Woman, due largely to Friedan's efforts. The UN had sanctioned the first international conference for women that same year, which was held in Mexico City and attended by six thousand representatives from over eighty countries. Friedan organized some of the conference's committee meetings, which provided the first forum in which women from Islamic, Communist, Zionist, democratic, apartheid, dictatorial, and demagogue nations had gathered to discuss women's issues. Title IX, which prohibited sex discrimination in school and college admissions, scholarships, and sports programs, was passed in 1972. The Supreme Court issued its *Roe v. Wade* decision, ruling that women could legally choose an abortion in the first term of pregnancy, in 1973. Friedan had been invited as one of the guests to sit in the visitor's gallery as the case was being heard. The Equal Credit Opportunity Act, which allowed a woman to get a credit card or car loan in her own name, had been signed into law in 1974. Sex-segregated "Help Wanted" ads had finally been ruled illegal, which opened hundreds of jobs to women, including police work, truck driving, fire fighting, airline piloting, and construction laboring. Women could no longer be prohibited from sitting on juries thanks to the Supreme Court's *Taylor v. Louisiana* decision, and all four branches of the armed forces integrated their ranks with women for the first time in 1976. Lawsuits against several major corporations had successfully forced them to acknowledge and take steps to rectify discrimination against women.

Continuing the momentum, Catherine East, Kay Clarenbach, Gloria Steinem, and Bella Abzug organized the First National Women's Conference in 1977. It was to be the first government-funded women's convention. One hundred thirty thousand women attended preparatory meetings in each state to draft recommendations and elect delegates to represent them at the conference.

Three First Ladies—Lady Bird Johnson, Betty Ford and Rosalyn Carter—two thousand voting delegates, and twenty thousand women attended the conference. The organizers appointed Friedan as a delegate-at-large and included her in the torch-lighting ceremony that opened the conference. The ceremony symbolized the link between Seneca Falls, New York, where Elizabeth Cady Stanton and Lucretia Mott had held the first women's rights convention in 1848, and Houston, Texas, the site of the First National Women's Conference in 1977. Issues on the conference agenda, called "planks," included child abuse, child care, battered women, homemakers' rights, employment, credit, health care, education, minority women, older women, reproductive freedom, rape, sexual preference, the ERA, nuclear weapons, and military spending. At this time, women still earned only fifty-nine cents for every dollar a man earned.

The conference was almost sidelined by the lesbian rights issue until Friedan decided to reverse her long-standing position and second a resolution to support the sexual preference plank. She said:

> I am considered to be violently opposed to the lesbian issue in the women's movement, and I have been. This issue has been used to divide us and disrupt us and has been seized on by our enemies to try and turn back the whole women's movement to equality, and alienate our support. As a woman of middle age who grew up in Middle America—in Peoria, Illinois—and who has loved men maybe too well, I have my personal hang-ups on this issue. I

Betty marching in Houston in 1977 with young activists Peggy Kokernot and Michelle Cearcy. *(©Diana Mara Henry, 1978.)*

have made mistakes. We have all made mistakes in our focus on this issue. But now we must all transcend our previous differences to devote our full energies to get the Equal Rights Amendment ratified, or we will lose all we have gained. . . . we must support the separate civil rights of our lesbian sisters.

The effect Friedan's change of position had on some feminists is summed up by Alix Kates Shulman, who wrote, "I was moved to tears when you delivered your speech in support of the sexual preference resolution. All around me women held their breath and felt the tears overflow as you said you had made a mistake (the same mistake made by so many). It meant so much to have you, the Mover, once again take an irrevocable step toward what we all desire; to see you move to close the wound, putting yourself, as always, in jeopardy for the sake of all of us." Friedan's move had ended the debate, which allowed the conference to continue on track and the delegates to adopt a far-reaching platform, a twenty-five-point *Plan of Action.*

As 1977 drew to a close, Friedan was pulling together her thoughts for a third book. Her second, titled *It Changed My Life,* had been published in 1976, almost twelve years after the contract was first negotiated and two years after it was renegotiated with an additional $25,000 advance. *It Changed My Life* was a reissue of the magazine articles, columns, and speeches Friedan had written during the early years of the movement. It did not sell well and was panned by most feminists who called it self-centered and self-righteous. The president of Random House Publishing Company had received a letter signed by twenty-six members of the NWPC. They claimed the book was "too marred by factual errors, self-serving fiction, racist assumptions and character assassinations of almost every nationally-known feminist or feminist organization to serve as any factual source on the women's movement or on the spirit or ideas of feminism." Nonetheless, Summit Books at Simon & Schuster gave Friedan a $100,000 advance and a contract for her third book.

In this book, Friedan planned to incorporate the findings of a think tank (a group organized to research and solve problems) she presided over in 1974. Friedan's think tank had been formed to explore new ways of addressing issues in the workplace in response to the 1974 recession. The recession had hit women the hardest because they were the last hired and therefore the first fired when jobs were cut. Friedan's think tank had studied new concepts to counter such actions and protect the inroads women had made in the workplace, including job sharing, overtime and compensatory time, four-day work weeks instead of five, parental leaves for both men and women, and guaranteed child care.

Friedan also planned to address an issue she had discovered while a visiting professor at Temple University in Philadelphia. There, Friedan encountered women who were trying to live the new equality but finding it difficult to manage a full-time job outside the home with the full-time job of mother. She saw husbands who wanted to be more hands-on, in-the-home fathers.

In addition to an exploration of these findings in her book, Friedan intended to write about the direction she thought the women's movement needed to take next. She called it the second stage. The first stage was finished, she argued. It had resulted in women and men finally being able to break out of sexually stereotyped male and female roles. The second stage, she believed, required a change in how men, women, and society defined and structured the home and the workplace so that men and women could enjoy equal opportunities in both places.

The Second Stage was published in 1981. Friedan admitted it was the fastest she had ever written a book. She was driven to get it out before the 1982 ratification deadline for the ERA. She hoped it would influence the outcome. The book received mixed reviews. Webster Schott's review in the *Washington Post* said, "Betty Friedan's *The Second Stage* is the right book at the right time. . . . [It] is intelligent, compassionate, and pertinent. It's an education. And it provides a course of action, especially for men. If we don't want for our mothers, wives and daughters the freedom we have, why is it worth having? If we are not partners with women, what are we?" Mary Cantwell wrote in her review for *Vogue,* "In *The Feminine Mystique,* Ms. Friedan spoke to the mainstream; in *The Second Stage,* she is the mainstream....When Ms. Friedan is discussing, wisely and well, how American thinking must be restructured towards flextime, parental leaves, and guaranteed child care, she is proceeding from the realities of modern American life."

Betty with two of her books, in 1980. *(Courtesy of The Schlesinger Library, Radcliffe Institute, Harvard University.)*

Others were more critical. Some argued that Betty was finally stating what they had been advocating all along. Others disagreed with her premise that the movement needed to be more inclusive of family life, believing this encouraged traditional roles and supported the notion that a woman needed a man to make a family.

The unraveling of her affair with David White, which followed the mediocre reception of her book, left Friedan deeply unsettled. She was also reeling from the surprise party her friends had thrown for her sixtieth birthday: "I could have killed them all . . . insisting as they did that I publicly acknowledge reaching sixty, pushing me out of life, as it seemed, out of the race. . . . I was depressed for weeks after that birthday party. . . . I could not face being sixty."

Friedan decided to go in a new direction and accepted a fellowship at the Institute of Politics at Harvard University's John F. Kennedy School of Government. The university provided her with a nineteenth-floor apartment overlooking the campus and the Charles River. She decorated it in her eclectic style with odd pieces of furniture, colorful Indian and Moroccan rugs, and a screen featuring a Haitian jungle scene.

Besides the opportunity to teach a course titled "Transcending Sexual Politics," Friedan was drawn to the position at Harvard because the university had offered her the use of all its resources. Friedan wanted to resume work on a fourth book and needed Harvard's rich source of research materials.

Chapter Eight

Confronting the Age Mystique

Friedan's fourth book idea evolved from a luncheon she had in 1978 with Dr. Robert Butler, a gerontologist (someone who specializes in the study of aging and its effects). Dr. Butler was the first to introduce the concept of "ageism," or discrimination against middle-aged and elderly people. He was the head of the National Institute on Aging and a recipient of the Pulitzer Prize for his book, *Why Survive?*, which was an exposé of the terrible treatment older people in America often received.

Dr. Butler had identified two issues that primarily affected aging women: Social Security and Medicare. To be eligible for Social Security and Medicare benefits, a person's employer must have forwarded a percentage of her paycheck to the Social Security Administration for ten years before she turned sixty-five. Women who spent their lives working in the home for zero wages were not entitled to these retirement benefits in their own names and had to gain access through their husband's benefits.

Dr. Butler had contacted Friedan because he was concerned that the women's movement was not addressing these issues. Statistics showed that American women lived eight years longer then men and comprised over sixty-five percent of the elderly population. Dr. Butler thought that if Friedan wrote about these problems, her reputation and prominence could get them on the public policy agenda.

Friedan began her Harvard research in earnest in 1982. She was amazed to discover that the university had no information or studies on the subject of aging. She started digging elsewhere and found similar results. What information she did uncover was based on research conducted in Alzheimer facilities and nursing homes. This triggered Friedan's inner Geiger counter and a sense of *déjà vu* from her research days for the Smith questionnaire and *The Feminine Mystique.* In both instances, those who were not affected were the ones defining the issues. In the case of women, it had been men who defined the problem. In the case of the elderly, it was young doctors who defined the problems associated with aging. They saw aging as a time of sickness, deterioration, helplessness, senility, incontinence, and childlike or dependent behavior. Friedan found this utterly horrifying, especially now that she was one of the indistinguishable group these experts were describing.

The Fountain of Age, as she eventually titled the book, would take Friedan ten years to finish. She would conduct hundreds of interviews with doctors, nursing home staffs, retirement center employees, government agency representatives, and the elderly themselves. One of her most important interviews would be with her own mother, who was in her mid-eighties and living in a retirement center in Laguna Hills, California. The interview deepened their relationship and allowed Friedan to finally come to terms with her mother.

Miriam Goldstein showed Betty that old age could be a time of renewed vitality and dimension. "I greatly admired her courage and her determined energy to live well," said Friedan. "I was able to put my arms around her and say, 'I love you, Mother,' and mean it. And she said, 'I know you do, darling, and I love you too.'"

Friedan continued traveling, teaching, and lecturing on the issues set forth in *The Second Stage* while she researched her book on aging. The women's movement had continued to make legislative and social progress since the early 1980s, and American women were making achievements never before considered possible. For the first time, a woman had moved up the ranks to become Brigadier General in the U.S. Air Force. She was General Wilma L. Vaught. The first woman, Sandra Day O'Connor, had been appointed to the United States Supreme Court, and Sally Ride became the first woman astronaut to travel into space.

The National Women's History Project (NWHP) was founded in 1980, and one of its early successes was to secure Presidential Recognition and a Congressional Resolution to designate March as National Women's History Month. The Supreme Court had ruled that sexual harassment in the workplace was illegal, and the Fair

Housing Act insured that women could no longer be discriminated against when it came to the sale, lease, or purchase of a home. In spite of these successes, however, the ERA failed to be ratified. It fell three states shy of the required thirty-eight.

Friedan was hugely disappointed and alarmed by the ERA's failure. It had seemed certain to be ratified after Congress passed it by a 354 to twenty-three vote in the House and an eighty-four to eight vote in the Senate in 1972. Within one year, thirty states had ratified it and by 1977, the number had increased to thirty-five. But the political climate in America had changed drastically after the formation of well-organized, well-connected political action groups like the Eagle Forum, the National Conservative Political Action Committee, and the Moral Majority (a political action group comprised of conservative fundamentalist Christians). The Moral Majority, for example, lobbied for prayer and the teaching of creationism in public schools and opposed the ERA, homosexual rights, and the Supreme Court's *Roe v. Wade* decision. These political action groups played a significant role in bringing to prominence the New Right, which began electing large numbers of conservative Republican candidates to Congress. They also helped elect Ronald Reagan president in 1980.

Friedan was equally troubled by the stagnation she saw in the "post-feminist generation" while on her lecture tours. The post-feminist generation was the generation of young women who were struggling with the new problems and pressures of balancing their professional careers with their desires to have and raise children. Balancing the dual roles of involved mother and successful career-woman was a difficult task. These younger women were struggling with these problems individually instead of collectively and politically. Many thought the women's movement had cheated them by making it seem that they could, and should, do it all. Once again, Friedan's inner Geiger counter went off.

Friedan was determined to show that these problems were political, not personal. She thought the new generation should see that society needed to press for political changes. She thought these changes should include meaningful child care programs, flexible work hours, shorter work weeks, equal pay for work of equal value, and equal Social Security benefits for women who chose to stay out of the workforce to take care of their children and homes. Friedan was alarmed to see that instead of working on these issues, the women's movement had been sidetracked with issues such as pornography that she thought were superfluous. Friedan began aggressively campaigning, lecturing, speaking, and writing on these second-stage solutions while she continued her research on aging at the Andrus Gerontology Center at the University of Southern California (USC).

In 1985, the American Jewish Congress sent Friedan and Bella Abzug to Nairobi for the third UN International Conference for Women. These conferences had been convened every five years following the first one Friedan had helped organize in 1975 in Mexico City. Seventeen thousand women from 159 nations attended.

A wide variety of women's issues were addressed in Nairobi. Arab, African, and Asian women asked how they were to begin going public with their desire to have fewer children without being ostracized by their religions and cultures. Some women from polygamous cultures wondered how they could ask their husbands to have only one wife. Others talked about how to keep moving ahead when events in their countries continually relegated women's concerns to the back burner.

Friedan was ecstatic that "a decade that began in acrimony in Mexico ended with success in Africa." At the same time, she was discouraged that the rest of the world seemed determined to continue making progress while the American movement seemed to be going backwards. There were, she realized, countries in Africa who had managed to include an equal rights clause in their constitutions while the United States still argued over it.

In 1986, Friedan decided to move part-time to southern California because the weather there provided some relief from the asthma she had been plagued with her entire life. She started another think tank at the University of Southern California. It lasted seven years and involved a variety of people in discussions about how the new equality for women was affecting women, men, family, work, and public policy. Many of Friedan's second-stage programs were discussed, as well as the need for research on how a child's development is affected by having an actively involved, in-the-home father—not only on what happens to a child whose mother works outside the home.

Friedan also received a greeting from Gloria Steinem in 1986, wishing her a happy sixty-fifth birthday. Steinem wrote, "I thank you for always being there. I thank you for giving all of us the gifts of your energy and caring. . . . When I passed fifty, I realized that fifty is what forty used to be. But watching you, I think that sixty-five is now what forty used to be. I wish you a long life and the great pleasure of seeing the difference you have made for so many." Friedan wrote Steinem a similar letter, and some years later, acknowledged Steinem's contributions to the women's movement.

In 1988, Friedan and Nancy Woodhull, founding editor of *USA Today,* put together a three-day seminar, "Women, Men and Media." Their seminar evolved from Friedan's USC think tank discussions, from a course she developed and taught at Harvard Business School called "Women, Men and Management," and from another course she taught at USC's School of Journalism, "Women, Men and Media." Friedan and Woodhull decided to continue their seminar as an ongoing, monitoring enterprise and dubbed it "Betty Friedan's Media Watch." Annually, they published a study of how women were represented and presented in the media. Their efforts had a significant impact. Television network newscasts where women were the subjects or focus of interviews increased; harmful stereotypes of women in advertising declined; the number of women in newsgathering and reporting roles went up; and women and women's issues finally found meaningful copy space on the front pages of major newspapers.

As rewarding as she found this enterprise and her work to promote the second stage of the women's movement, Friedan knew she had to focus on writing her book about aging. She had been researching for six years when she went to Sag Harbor (an old whaling town in the Hamptons, NY) in the summer of 1988 and tried to set up a work routine. Friedan had purchased a home there in 1978. It was a lovely, two-story, white clapboard house with black shutters that had been built in 1820. Friedan worked on her books during the summer and taught and lectured during the remaining months.

Friedan settled into a routine that allowed her to write for five or six hours a day and spend the rest of her time recharging. Writing books was a chore for her. She hated the feeling of never being done, unlike the gratification she had experienced with writing magazine articles. She still didn't use a computer or typewriter. She had written everything since the second chapter of *The Feminine Mystique* by hand on a yellow tablet. After four agonizing summers, she finally finished *The Fountain of Age* in 1992. "I was positively euphoric," she said. She was seventy-one years old.

Friedan was hospitalized just six months before the book's publication. What she thought had been an asthma attack was actually an infected aortic valve in her heart. She needed immediate open-heart surgery. All three of her children and her ex-husband Carl were at her bedside. As she was wheeled into surgery she found herself reciting the *Shema Yisrel* to calm her anxiety. Friedan's body rejected the replacement pig valve, which was a common replacement before the development of artificial valves. She joked, "What good Jewish heart wouldn't reject pork?" Friedan went in for a second surgery with only a fifty-fifty chance of survival. Within weeks, she was promoting her new book before the American Booksellers Association Convention in Miami, Florida. Though she was in a wheelchair due to her weakened condition, her voice and delivery were as strong as ever.

The Fountain of Age stayed on the *New York Times* Best-Seller List for six weeks. Almost every Sunday newspaper's magazine carried a profile of Friedan and a review of her new book.

In her book Friedan revealed that most of the research on aging depicted age as a time of regret and decrepitude. Society was still stuck on old notions about aging, even as life expectancy continued to rise. At the turn of the twentieth century men were expected to live to forty-five and women to forty-six. By the early 1990s, an average man might live to seventy and women regularly lived to seventy-eight. As people lived longer, healthier lives, the entire concept of aging had to change.

Friedan urged her readers to rethink old age, to see it not as a threat or something to be denied, but as a different stage of life. She urged her readers to stop longing for their youth and suggested that instead they enjoy this new part of their lives and embrace the changes that came with it. She pointed out that there are advantages to age just as there are to youth. As one reviewer for the *Washington Post* wrote, "[This book] will liberate us from the tyranny of youth as surely as *The Feminine Mystique* liberated women from the calcified gender role of mother/sex object. . . . She torpedoes the cultural fixation on infirmities of old age."

The summer of 1993 was the first in twenty-five years that Friedan did not have a looming book deadline. Her three children, their spouses, and her eight grandchildren descended on the Sag Harbor home they called Grandmere's house. She loved watching her grandchildren scramble to stake their claims on cots and sleeping bags in the loft, and spending lazy days with them, swimming and combing the beach. Everyone would crowd around the long wooden table that filled the kitchen to enjoy casual dinners and lively conversations that lasted well into the evenings.

Friedan and Carl had reconciled to the extent that they now celebrated holidays and family events together in Sag Harbor with all the kids and grandkids. They had a great deal to make them proud. All three children had graduated with professional degrees—Jonathan was an engineer, Daniel a physicist, and Emily a physician, and all three were enjoying success in their private and professional lives.

Discovering that her asthma had disappeared in the months following her heart surgery, Friedan accepted an offer to become an adjunct scholar at the Woodrow Wilson International Center for Scholars in Washington, D.C. instead of returning to California. She was thrilled to find an elegant apartment in D.C., a city she enjoyed for its political and social importance and influence.

Her work at the Wilson Center involved co-chairing symposia on women, men, work, family, and public policy with Heidi Hartmann, an economist and founder of the Institute for Women's Policy Research. Every four weeks the two women brought together representatives from labor, corporate America, Congress, and other public policy makers to address the new questions coming to light in the 1990s. They dealt with "the upsurge of 'angry white men' in the epidemic of corporate downsizing and dropping incomes; [and] the bitter scapegoating of women and minorities which was forming a new backlash." They also discussed what to do about the overload of work being imposed on the smaller workforce and the increased stress on couples and parents caused by the loss of personal time.

Possible solutions were adequate parental leave for both parents and flexible working hours. Another idea was to do more to help divorced or unemployed women, often with young children, who wanted to finish school, find another job, or participate in job-training programs. There were lengthy discussions regarding the need for society to view parenting and household duties not just as the mother's responsibility, but as the father's equal responsibility as well.

Eventually, Friedan and a visiting fellow at Mount Vernon College in Washington, Brigid O'Farrell, co-wrote *Beyond Gender: The New Politics of Work and Family.* It was based on the findings gleaned from these Wilson Center symposia. The book was published by the Wilson Center Press and was well received by its largely academic audience.

Friedan continued her involvement with feminist issues on the international level. She attended the UN's Fourth World Conference for Women in Beijing in 1995. Forty thousand women attended—almost seven times the number that had attended the first conference in 1975. These international conferences always left Friedan feeling revitalized.

Her focus narrowed in 1997, however, after she survived emergency open-heart surgery to replace her disintegrated heart valve with a mechanical one. She was seventy-six years old and realized that her life could not go on indefinitely. She decided to concentrate on the things dearest to her—her family and her work. As always, it could not be one or the other; she valued these two parts of her life equally.

Friedan started taking each of her grandchildren on a trip, one by one, to places like Cuba, France, and the Galapagos Islands. In between trips, she continued her work on second-stage issues. To that end, Friedan approached the Ford Foundation and Cornell University for support. She was given a distinguished professorship at Cornell in 1998, which in turn received a one million-dollar grant from the Ford Foundation to fund Friedan's work. She also began writing her sixth book, an autobiography.

Life So Far was published in the year 2000, thirty-seven years after Friedan's catalytic work, *The Feminine Mystique.* She was seventy-nine years old. Through a recounting of her life in the book and in subsequent interviews and articles, Friedan cautioned readers and listeners to recognize that in spite of the huge advances women had made, there was still much unfinished business. For instance, seventy-eight percent of families with children had two parents working outside the home, yet the workplace was still structured around a working father and a stay-at-home mother. Women were providing fifty percent or more of the income in fifty percent or more of American households, yet, on average, they earned seventy-four cents to a man's dollar. This was primarily the result of women choosing flexible jobs and lower salaries in order to be more available to their children during child-rearing years. Friedan urged her readers and listeners to concentrate on helping women and men to combine work and families through social and political changes, namely a national child care program, paid family leave, and equal sharing of household and child rearing responsibilities by men and women.

To explain why she had dedicated the last half of her life to feminist issues, Friedan wrote in *Life So Far,* "I did it for my father in a way, so that men would not have the burden of their wives' frustration at having to live through them. I did it for my mother, so that women would no longer have the discontent of dependency on their husbands, with no careers of their own. And I did it for my children, so that children would not have the burden of the mothers having to live through them."

Betty Friedan was able to use her life experiences to transform society. Her own words do the best job of expressing this: "Whatever experiences I've had in my life—my education that I never thought I used in a real

career, my mother's frustration which I finally understood, my learning experiences as a journalist in the labor
movement, getting fired for pregnancy, freelancing for
women's magazines in the 'happy housewife' era, . . . the
lasting joys as well as the regrets of my marriage, my
aging—all of this I've used finally. I have used it all. Who
knows how I'll use it next?"

Timeline

1921   Born in Peoria, Illinois on February 4.

1934-   Attends Central High School; writes for school newspa-
1938   per, *Opinion;* co-founds school's first literary magazine,
        Tide.

1938-   Attends Smith College; graduates *summa cum laude;*
1942   Editor-in-chief of *Smith College Associated News (SCAN);*
        college thesis published in *Psychological Review.*

1942   Enters the University of California at Berkeley to study
        for a Master's degree in Psychology.

1943   Awarded the Abraham Rosenberg Research Fellowship,
        but turns it down; moves to New York City to work as a
        labor journalist for *Federated Press.*

1944   Enters psychoanalysis.

1945   Marries Carl Friedman on June 12.

1948   Daniel (Danny) Friedan born on October 3.

1952   Fired for being pregnant; Jonathan Friedan is born on No-
        vember 27.

1953   Returns to writing; changes name to Betty Friedan.

1956   Emily Friedan born on May 23.

1963   Publishes *The Feminine Mystique.*

1966   Co-founds National Organization for Women (NOW); named president of the organization.

1969   Co-founds National Association for the Repeal of Abortion Laws (NARAL); divorces Carl.

1970   Leads the first women's rights demonstration and march on August 26.

1971   Co-founds National Women's Political Caucus (NWPC).

1973   Begins a ten-year affair with David Manning White.

1976   Publishes *It Changed My Life.*

1981   Publishes *The Second Stage.*

1988   Co-creates "Betty Friedan's Media Watch."

1993   Publishes *The Fountain of Age.*

1998   Accepts Distinguished Professorship at Cornell University.

2000   Publishes her autobiography, *Life So Far.*

Sources

CHAPTER ONE: Growing Up a Golstein

p. 11, "Now I lay me down . . ." Betty Friedan, *Life So Far* (New York: Simon & Schuster, 2001), 15.

p. 11, "[a] boy that likes . . ." Ibid.

p. 12, "why she made our life . . ." Ibid.

p. 15, "She married him because . . ." Judith Hennessee, *Betty Friedan, Her Life* (New York: Viking, 1999), 5.

p. 16, "Our mother always looked . . ." Ibid., 7.

p. 16, "she did perfectly . . ." Friedan, *Life So Far,* 16.

p. 19, "At the dinner table . . ." Ibid., 19.

p. 20, "My mother, to . . ." Ibid., 18.

p. 20, "she never had anything . . ." Ibid., 16.

p. 21, "the rest of the family . . ." Ibid., 19.

p. 21, "At school I came . . ." Ibid.

p. 21, "School was my safe place . . ." Ibid., 20.

p. 22, "I wasn't good at . . ." Ibid., 19.

p. 22, "Nothing I did was ever right . . ." Ibid.

CHAPTER TWO: Lonely in Peoria

p. 24, "created a kind of . . ." Friedan, *Life So Far,* 19.

p. 25, "as my mother made . . ." Ibid., 22.
p. 25, "I loved hanging around that theater," Ibid.
p. 25, "I've decided I don't . . ." Ibid.
p. 25, "keep it to [her]self . . ."Ibid.
p. 25, "I soulfully raised . . ." Ibid.
p. 26, "were getting breasts . . ." Ibid., 24.
p. 26, "I would walk . . ." Ibid., 24-25.
p. 27, "My mother didn't want . . ." Ibid., 24.
p. 27, "They may not like me . . ." Ibid., 25.
p. 28, "It was not very useful to be . . ." Ibid.
p, 29, "We would walk up Main . . ." Ibid.
p. 29, "I cannot remember ever . . ." Ibid., 31.
p. 30, "Literally, physically, she . . ." Ibid., 30-31.
p. 30, "When Betty was in high . . ." Hennessee, *Betty Friedan,* 14.
p. 32, "inordinately ambitious . . ." Daniel Horowitz, *Betty Friedan and the Making of the Feminine Mystique, The American Left, The Cold War, and Modern Feminism* (Amherst: University of Massachusetts Press, 1998), 32.
p. 32, "I want to do something . . ." Ibid.
p. 32, "She made it possible . . ." Friedan, *Life So Far,* 32.
p. 32, "it was seared deep in . . ." Ibid., 30.

CHAPTER THREE: Coming into Her Own
p. 34, "passionately arguing in . . ." Friedan, *Life So Far,* 37.
p. 34, "the academic life . . ." Ibid.
p. 38, "My father's friends . . ." Hennessee, *Betty Friedan,* 28.
p. 40, "Whatever came to her attention . . ." Ibid., 23.
p. 40, "She was bossy, but I did . . ." Ibid.
p. 40, "I loved walking home from . . ." Friedan, *Life So Far,* 42.
p. 40, "It fascinated me . . ." Ibid., 47.
p. 40, "either a hopeless . . ." Ibid.
p. 41, "the elegant conceptual . . ." Ibid., 45.
p. 43, "I was that girl . . ." Horowitz, *Betty Friedan and the Making of the Feminine Mystique,* 86.

p. 43, "I remember the . . ." Betty Friedan, *The Feminine Mystique,* Revised Edition (New York: Bantam Doubleday Dell Publishing Group, Inc., 1983), 69.

p. 44, "Nobody had ever really . . ." Friedan, *Life So Far,* 47.

CHAPTER FOUR: Radical Reporter

p. 49, "For us, the . . ." Friedan, *Life So Far,* 57.

p. 51, "he took [her] to real . . ." Ibid., 59.

p. 51, "He seemed an old man . . ." Ibid., 61.

p. 52, "You can take that fellowship . . ." Hennessee, *Betty Friedan,* 36.

p. 52, "if I took that fellowship . . ." Friedan, *Life So Far,* 62.

p. 54, "I remember the . . ." Ibid., 71-72.

p. 56, "I never could explain . . ." Hennessee, *Betty Friedan,* 38.

p. 56, "learned about the evils . . ." Friedan, *Life So Far,* 40.

p. 59, "the vanguard of . . ." Horowitz, *Betty Friedan and the Making of the Feminine Mystique,* 122.

p. 59, "very political . . ." Ibid.

p. 59, "He brought me an . . ." Friedan, *Life So Far,* 67.

p. 61, "My mother had no love to give . . ." Hennessee, *Betty Friedan,* 44.

p. 62, "I was lonely in the . . ." Ibid., 47.

p. 62, "we always . . ." Friedan, *Life So Far,* 70.

p. 62, "equality of sacrifice . . ." Horowitz, *Betty Friedan and the Making of the Feminine Mystique,* 137.

p. 62, "[where is] the morality of one . . ." Ibid.

CHAPTER FIVE: Suburban Housewife and Mother

p. 65, "At that time in my life . . ." Friedan, *Life So Far,* 76.

p. 65, "A great deal of my . . ." Hennessee, *Betty Friedan,* 51.

p. 67, "an elucidation of the . . ." Friedan, *Life So Far,* 72.

p. 67, "the insight that, unlike other . . ." Ibid., 73.

p. 68, "After the loneliness of war . . ." Friedan, *The Feminine Mystique,* 182-83.

p. 69, "It's your fault . . ." Friedan, *Life So Far,* 79.

p. 71, "Why are you pretending . . ." Ibid., 82.

p. 74, "happy, fulfilled . . ." Ibid., 85.

p. 74, "I seem to remember . . ." Ibid., 87.

p. 76, "Women...have a unique opportunity . . ." Ibid., 98.

p. 77, "It was more important . . ." Ibid., 96.

p. 79, "Betty has always . . ." Ibid., 103.

p. 79, "'I'm Jim's wife . . ." Ibid., 104.

CHAPTER SIX: Launching a Revolution

p. 83, "The problem lay buried . . ." Friedan, *The Feminine Mystique,* 15.

p. 87, "Oh, sex discrimination?. . ." Friedan, *Life So Far,* 170.

p. 88, "down the road . . ." Ibid., 163.

p. 89, "Nobody ever appointed . . ." Ibid., 167-68.

p. 92, "the groundwork . . ." Ibid., 174.

p. 93, "to take the actions . . ." Horowitz, *Betty Friedan and the Making of the Feminine Mystique,* 227.

p. 94, "She sweeps through . . ." Ibid., 229-30.

p. 94, "We may only have . . ." Friedan, *Life So Far,* 182.

p. 95, "I felt gooseflesh . . ." Ibid., 206.

p. 95, "to hold a national . . ." Ibid., 199.

p. 97, "it's been with breathless . . ." Ibid., 164.

p. 98, "I am for the . . ." Hennessee, *Betty Friedan,* 240.

CHAPTER SEVEN: Defeats and Victories

p. 100, "Betty's greatest strength . . ." Horowitz, *Betty Friedan and the Making of the Feminine Mystique,* 230.

p, 100, "I have led you into . . ." Hennessee, *Betty Friedan,* 135.

p. 102, "did everything and anything . . ." Ibid., 165.

p. 103, "People didn't want . . ." Ibid., 168.

p. 103, "People didn't trust . . ." Ibid.

p. 104, "It was a huge battle . . ." Ibid., 188-89.

p. 107, "countless discussions . . ." Friedan, *Life So Far,* 278.

p. 107, "'Sin began with a woman . . .'" Ibid., 279.

p. 107, "I bring you this . . ." Ibid.

p. 108, "He took my hands . . ." Ibid., 280.

p. 108, "It didn't matter . . ." Hennessee, *Betty Friedan,* 192.

p. 109, "I couldn't fulfill all . . ." Ibid., 224-25.

p. 112, "I am considered to . . ." Ibid., 234-35.

p. 114, "I was moved to tears when . . ." Ibid., 235.

p. 115, "too marred by factual errors . . ." Ibid., 218.

p. 116, "Betty Friedan's *The Second Stage . . .*" Ibid., 240.

p. 116, "In *The Feminine . . .*" Ibid.

p. 118, "I could have killed . . ." Ibid., 243.

CHAPTER EIGHT: Confronting the Age Mystique

p. 121, "I greatly admired . . ." Friedan, *Life So Far,* 348.

p. 121, "I was able . . ." Hennessee, *Betty Friedan,* 259.

p. 124, "a decade that began in acrimony . . ." Ibid., 250.

p. 125, "I thank you for always . . ." Ibid., 252.

p. 126, "I was positively . . ." Friedan, *Life So Far,* 349.

p. 127, "What good Jewish . . ." Ibid., 353.

p. 127, "[This book] will liberate . . ." Hennessee, *Betty Friedan,* 273-74.

p. 129, "the upsurge of . . ." Friedan, *Life So Far,* 358.

p. 131, "I did it for my . . ." Ibid., 378.

p. 132, "Whatever experiences I've . . ." Ibid., 380.

Bibliography

Davis, Flora. *Moving the Mountain, The Women's Movement in America Since 1960.* Urbana and Chicago: University of Illinois Press, 1999.

Friedan, Betty. Edited by Brigid O'Farrell. *Beyond Gender: The New Politics of Work and Family.* Washington, D.C.: The Woodrow Wilson Center Press, 1997.

———. *The Feminine Mystique,* Revised Edition. New York: Bantam Doubleday Dell Publishing Group, Inc., 1983.

———. *Life So Far.* New York: Simon & Schuster, 2001.

———. *The Second Stage,* Revised Edition. New York: Summit Books, 1986.

Hennessee, Judith. *Betty Friedan, Her Life.* New York: Viking, 1999.

Horowitz, Daniel. *Betty Friedan and the Making of the Feminine Mystique, The American Left, The Cold War, and Modern Feminism.* Amherst: University of Massachusetts Press, 1998.

Web sites

National Organization for Women (NOW)
www.now.org
The official Web site of the organization Betty Friedan helped to found, it offers the group's history as well as news of current events and issues.

National Women's Hall of Fame
www.greatwomen.org
Honoring American women who have contributed to the arts, athletics, business, education, government, the humanities, philanthropy, and science.

National Women's History Project (NWHP)
www.nwhp.org
The organization's official Web site, featuring a wealth of information on the group's history and ongoing projects.

Women in American History by Encyclopædia Britannica
www.britannica.com/women/index.html
Covers American women's history from the 1600s through the present, with bios, timelines, essays, recommended reading lists, and links.

Index